Dispatches: Turning Points in Theology and Global Crises

Dispatches: Turning Points in Theology and Global Crises draws on the legacy of early twentieth-century theological responses to the crises of the two world wars. During World War II, the Signposts series (Dacre Press, 1940) sought to offer an interruption of a theological malaise in the midst of mass violence and destruction. Contributors from that series, including Julian Casserley, Eric Mascall, and Donald Mac-Kinnon, among others, offered slim volumes that drew from diverse resources and harnessed the apocalyptic political urgency of the dialectical school within the theological grammar of a more traditional Anglo-Catholic Thomism. Similarly, and inspired significantly by MacKinnon's contributions, this present series draws on diverse theological resources in order to offer urgent responses to contemporary crises.

While the title of the series conveys the digest nature of the volumes, the subtitle, Turning Points, indicates the apocalyptic urgency of the issues addressed, and yet reserves any prescriptive judgment on the manner in which the tradition can be reappropriated by our authors. In this way, we seek to offer a genuinely creative and disruptive theological-ethical *ressourcement* for church in the present moment. With conceptual agility and faithfulness, this series will provide intelligent and yet accessible reflections on the shape and form of theological life in the present.

Dispatches will illuminate and explore, creatively and concisely, the implications and relevance of theology for the global crises of late modernity. Our authors have been invited to introduce succinct and provocative arguments intended to provoke dialogue and exchange of ideas, while setting in relief the implications of theology for political and moral life.

Series Editors

Ashley John Moyse (PhD, Newcastle) is the McDonald Post-doctoral Fellow in Christian Ethics and Public Life, Christ Church, University of Oxford.

Scott A. Kirkland (PhD, Newcastle) is the John and Jeane Stockdale Lecturer in Practical Theology and Ethics and research coordinator for the Trinity College Theological School, University of Divinity, Melbourne.

Published Titles

The End Is Not Yet by John W. de Gruchy
Political Orthodoxies by Cyril Hoverun
Theology and the Globalized Present by John C. McDowell
Theology, Comedy, Politics by Marcus Pound
The Art of Living for a Technological Age by Ashley John Moyse

Forthcoming Titles

Gender Violence Church by Anna Mercedes
Intersectionality, Religion, and Theology by Joerg Rieger

The Art of Living for a
Technological Age

The Art of Living for a Technological Age

Toward a Humanizing Performance

Ashley John Moyse

Fortress Press
Minneapolis

THE ART OF LIVNG FOR A TECHNOLOGICAL AGE
Toward a Humanizing Performance

Cover design: Alisha Lofgren
Cover illustration: © iStock 2020: Conceptual Max pointing at something by Pavel_R

Print ISBN: 978-1-5064-3163-5

Ebook ISBN: 978-1-5064-6919-5

To Theodore Karabo Moyse,
may you learn to become as discerning
as the bees.

For there are few things which the modern man . . .
needs to impress upon his mind . . . in order to remain
alive before God and for himself he must find a place for
rest, no matter what the cost. The strange thing is that in
spite of all the astonishing possibilities of intensification,
multiplication and acceleration which he has been able to
create for himself in the constantly mounting
development of his technical mastery of work, he has not
so far caused or allowed himself to be induced to relax, to
find relief and liberation, to be released from tension, to
find intelligent diversion and therefore to find the way to
true work. On the contrary, all these new possibilities
have thus far had only the result of setting an increasing
pace by the accelerating tempo of his machines and
gadgets, so that he is driven and chased and harried as it
were by them. He has let himself be set by them in a
mounting fever for work, and while this fever may later
prove to be a channel to new and better health, there is
also the possibility—and there are more pointers in this
direction—that the patient will one day die of it. There is
also the possibility that it is a symptom of the
approaching and gigantic ruin of at least a stage of
civilisation. There is also the possibility that it cannot
continue very much longer. We can scarcely maintain
that what modern man has so far achieved in this
increasing fever is either gratifying or hopeful.

—Karl Barth. *Church Dogmatics, Volume III. The Doctrine
of Creation, Part 4*. Translated by Geoffrey W. Bromiley and
Thomas F. Torrance. Edinburgh: T&T Clark, 2004, 555–56.

Contents

Acknowledgments

I am grateful to several people who have played an important role in the writing and publishing of *The Art of Living for a Technological Age*. First among them is my colleague and dear friend Scott A. Kirkland, who has been instrumental in preparing and advancing the series in which this volume is included. His attention to this volume in particular, with incisive comment and encouragement, has only made this a better book. I am also grateful to Michael Gibson for his friendly, adept, and professional support in bringing this series to press. And to the editorial team at Fortress Press, with special thanks to Will Bergkamp and Silas Morgan as well as Claire Brubaker and Marissa Wold Uhrina, I am grateful for the continued and careful attention to the series.

There are so many others who have contributed to this volume, as readers, conversation partners, commenters, and critics. They are a global network of friends, peers, and mentors, whose inclusion here reminds me that a human being is a being together—and academic work *can* be a communal event. To Michael Burdett, Scott Campbell, Ron Dart, Celia Deane-Drummond, Ross Hastings, Fabrice Jotterand, Mike Mawson, John McDowell, David Robinson, Aaron Walters, Brent Waters, and Jens Zimmermann, among many others: each of you has contributed to this volume, providing commentary and reflections, conversations and challenges. You have given of your time and your attention. For everything, I am fortunate. But it is your friendship that I appreciate most.

To my students back in Vancouver and here in Oxford, you've been a source of joy, laughter, and pride. To Lydia Corriveau, Sophia McLean, Paul Robinson, and Alex Trew: it has been a joy to journey with and to learn from you as you've each pursued important and challenging questions and as you've given attention to my own research and writing. You've all demonstrated humility, patience, charity, and good humor. And to Scout Brobst and Gemma Baker: I am honored to have had the opportunity to work with you both as you've pursued undergraduate and postgraduate studies, respectively. You have often been a source of great delight as I've watched you flourish. Moreover, your respective attention to and assistance with this project is appreciated greatly. And to Maria Beer Vuco, my research assistant: thank you. Your curiosity and competence, thoughtfulness and talents are commendable. I am honored to have such an affable and gifted scholar to work with and to learn from.

To my colleagues in Oxford, including Nigel Biggar, Dafydd Daniel, Carol Harrison, Joshua Hordern, Eleanor McLaughlin, and Graham Ward: I have deeply appreciated the opportunities for ranging conversations and good humor—oftentimes over fine food and good drink. Getting to know each of you has been a great joy. But to Nigel, Carol, and Graham: you've welcomed me into the McDonald Centre and to Christ Church with kindness and enthusiasm. I am fortunate to have such good mentors to learn with and from.

I am also indebted to the John Templeton Foundation, whose generous support resourced the early development of this project. And to the McDonald Agape Foundation, whose generosity has created an enduring legacy in Oxford, through which I am able to continue my work. The thoughts and opinions expressed in this project, however, are my own and do not necessarily reflect those of either the John Templeton Foundation or the McDonald Agape Foundation.

Finally, all of these expressions of gratitude pale in comparison to the appreciation and recognition, as well as time, that is owed to my family, Aime and Theo.

Ashley John Moyse
Christ Church, Oxford
Ordinary Time, 2020

Prologue: Encountering the Crisis

Before my current appointment, I had the privilege of taking up a research appointment and sessional lectureship at Vancouver School of Theology and a postdoctoral fellowship at Regent College in Vancouver. These positions resourced the time and space to read, to think, and to write, leading to several projects, including the genesis of this book. These positions demanded a range of responsibilities also, including the opportunity to engage with students in and outside the classroom. At one such experience, a panel discussion, I was invited to respond to a few student questions. The final question was phrased this way: Are there any technologies or uses of technologies that Christians should boldly condemn, and why?

I paused to gather my thoughts and to consider my response. Yet that was enough of a silence to allow the convener to jump in and draw the seminar, now in overtime, to a close.

But, as I was chased down outside the limited class setting, the student inquired again. I offered a curt response, which went something like this: I would condemn technologically enabled violence expressed, for example, by military aggression. I would encourage us to condemn industrial technologies of war, including smart rockets projected from naval warships and bombs released from intelligent drones toward so-called targets, as though one were aiming for the inanimate objects of a video game while discounting the human cost, whether innocent civilians or rival combatants. I would condemn the industries of war and the economic machinations that make killing profitable. I would condemn such technologies that bolster the powers of Death.

Why? An equally curt rationale followed: Death is revealed, in such acts, as a moral power, wielded by nation-states or militant groups to obtain particular ends and social purposes. It illuminates a particular technological rationality whereby domination, by military terror and triumph, guarantees economic and security advantage for those tied to, that is, dependent on, the corporate-military-industrial-complex that is increasingly interested in certain technologies, including contemporary advancements in robotics, artificial intelligence, and remote warfare. Yet such advantage is won, in the age of smart machines, without due attention to the human cost—"friends" operating unmanned aerial vehicles for intelligence or intervention who see and participate in the carnage of war, all in high definition from the so-called safety of remote locations, but no less traumatized by the power of Death; "enemies," whether civilian or combatant, cut down by Death's power, now promoted with the further guarantee of "precision warfare." Death allures by such foolish guarantees of domination and security (often introduced in the same breath as peace). And there are many who labor to justify war, and the killing of persons, accordingly. But in the face of Death, as a moral power, should we not learn to struggle toward living (whatever that might mean)? Should we not learn how to live humanly in the midst of and by dissenting Death, as William Stringfellow (1928–1985) invited his reader?[1]

Surely, we must try. Of course, this reveals a particular conviction that has nurtured postures of nonviolence and a commitment to pacificism, at very least.

Nevertheless, such a curt response and rationale, as offered above, might not have been heard well by the student. It might not be read well here either. Perhaps a tempered response to the question might be better. In fact, a tempered response to the student's question might provoke reflection instead of recoil.

Accordingly, I would encourage us to look beyond mere industrial technologies and consider both moral and political techniques, too. Accordingly, we must learn to discern techniques of any kind that instrumentalize human life, reducing human being to a brute materiality, a *bare life*, as Georgio Agamben has said.[2]

1. William Stringfellow, *An Ethic for Christians and Other Aliens in a Strange Land* (Eugene, OR: Wipf & Stock, 2004), 118–22.
2. Giorgio Agamben, *Homo Sacer: Sovereign Power and Bare Life*, trans. Daniel Heller-Roazen (Stanford: Stanford University Press, 1995).

I would condemn, with Michel Henry (1922–2002), the barbarous disposition wherein "Everything that can be done by science ought to be done by it and for it, since there is nothing but science and the reality that it names, namely objective reality."[3] Such a reality is one in which culture is lost, where dialogue and difference are replaced by monologue and homogeneity, where power to form usurps creativity, restraining the freedom, for life.

Therefore, I would also condemn technologies wherein, as Gabriel Marcel (1889–1973) forewarns, personality, particularity, and difference are amputated until "the situation of each of us becomes as similar as possible to that of [our] neighbour."[4] Marcel here is not speaking about issues of justice, but of the mechanized, rationalized, and bureaucratized situation that risks reducing all toward a particular order. George Ritzer might call this situation the McDonaldization of society, which ought to be condemned.[5] Thus, I would condemn those techniques where persons are reduced by the will to form, as Karl Barth (1886–1968) lamented.[6]

I would, consequently, contest those techniques, following after Frederick W. Taylor's (1856–1915) "scientific man-

3. Michel Henry, *Barbarism* (London: Continuum, 2012), 55.
4. Gabriel Marcel, *Man against Mass Society*, trans. G. S. Fraser (South Bend, IN: St. Augustine's, 2008), 19.
5. George Ritzer, *The McDonaldization of Society* (Los Angeles: Pine Forge, 2009).
6. Karl Barth, *Protestant Theology in the Nineteenth Century: Its Background and History*, trans. Brian Cozens and John Bowden (Grand Rapids: Eerdmans, 2002), 41.

agement,"[7] for example, that constrain human vocation and replace meaningful work (of any kind) with a type of dehumanizing measure that makes persons into the marketable and managed labor market.[8] Such markets are those where persons become replaceable as though they were mere cogs: nameless, faceless, meaningless—only meaningful for particular ends, useful only when performing the designated function; meaningful as a part delimited and bounded by the technological machinery and the powers of the market. I would contest the technocratic ideations of control over nature and over people that have forged economic programs (i.e., industrial capitalism) and political structures (i.e., corporate-military-industrial complex) that are complicit in the technological determining of the material structures of the world, and that define what is possible—specifically, what is possible for the perpetual progress and profit of economic programs and corporate structures themselves.[9]

In my book *Reading Karl Barth, Interrupting Moral Technique, Transforming Biomedical Ethics*, I confront the apparatus of the (secular) common morality incumbent to contemporary biomedical ethics, a moral technique, to be sure, that determines moral speech and cares little about the panoply and

7. Frederick Winslow Taylor, *Scientific Management: The Early Sociology of Management and Organizations*, vol. 1 (New York: Routledge, 2003). This volume includes "Shop Management" (1903), "The Principles of Scientific Management" (1911), and "Testimony before the Special House Committee" (1912).
8. Romano Guardini, *The End of the Modern World* (Wilmington, DE: ISI Books, 2013), 179.
9. David King, "Exposing Technocracy—The Mindset of Industrial Capitalism," *The Ecologist* (June 27, 2015), https://tinyurl.com/wank4od.

particularity of persons captured by crises of life and death. Instead I argue that we ought to demonstrate solidarity to persons, not principles, attending to actual crises that demand decision rather than a priori constructs that determine both questions and answers before the crisis. So we must refuse to set aside persons, neighbors both near and distant. We must refuse to abandon the peculiarity of theological ethics in favor of such moral apparatus when we gather at the ethics roundtable.

That said, answering such a question as I was asked was originally meant to participate in a pedagogical exercise. My response, I suppose, was intended to provoke further reflection. Perhaps both the curt and tempered responses have done just that already.

Of course, I cannot be sure.

Yet I am sure of this: that question sparked further thinking about technology and catalyzed attention toward the writing of this book.

I am also sure of this: the purpose of this book is to advance not only a critical reflection on our technological age but also an understanding of the ways in which we might participate in human becoming. It is a book, therefore, that might help us toward a form of ethical or humanizing performance that moves beyond the hegemony of our technological society and toward a kind of educative, and therefore transformative, material social practice.

The book will illuminate the meaning of technology while clarifying the crisis we must confront. It will elucidate the critical turning point that we are facing—and have been facing for some time—the crisis concerning the cosmogony of technology, that is, the reality it has created. It is a crisis that concerns our being (and becoming) human in and for our techno-evolving society. It concerns the "energies once hidden in the depths of nature,"[10] as Nicholas Berdyaev (1874–1948) puts it, but now active in a world of our making—a world at risk of deformation. It concerns the powers procured by our own creative agencies, but powers that are now wielded over nature, over other human persons, over life itself.[11] It is vital that we learn to see such a crisis for what it is and address it rightly. It is vital that we understand the essence of technology and of the freedom for human being.

This volume emerges from crises incumbent to those wrought from advancements and applications in modern sciences and technologies. It will turn our attention to the relationship that the questions above demand we explore. Therefore, follow me toward understanding the crisis, which positions this book in the Dispatches series: a series that aims to provoke dialogue and exchange of ideas, while setting in relief the implications of theology for crises that beleaguer the present age. Follow me also toward a theologi-

---

10. Nicholas Berdyaev, "Dukhovnoye sostoyaniye sovremennogo mira [*hereafter*, Spiritual Condition of the Modern World]," *Put* [The Way] 35 (1935): 56–68, here 59, https://tinyurl.com/wqdoz85 (translation mine).
11. Berdyaev, "Spiritual Condition of the Modern World," 59.

cal response that bears witness to a responsive (responsible) performance, or education, that cultivates human being in and for our technological age.

Ashley John Moyse
Christ Church, Oxford
Advent, 2019

PART I

Sketching the Crisis

1

The Fate of the Technological World

Writers often begin with a provocative first few sentences. This exercise makes sense for those who wish their readers to continue reading. It is a good technique. It might be an ideal technique to employ when setting out to write on the question and crisis of technology—it has, after all, proven a successful method, so perhaps I would be unwise to do differently.

The publisher, for instance, would surely prefer that this book sells many copies and is read widely.

Perhaps I have failed to execute the provocative introduction. In failing to do so, however, I may have accomplished two things (if readers have continued to read). First,

I may have captured attention by other means—speaking of provocation without giving in to the demand to be provocative. Second, I may have thwarted the powers of technique that so often constrain and homogenize human action, making it all the same, including the task of writing, exchanging sparks of creativity for efficiencies of form.

It is possible that I have succumbed to the technique ordered by the mechanics of writing by structuring the introduction of this volume as I have (and this might be why readers continue to read). Perhaps it would be correct to assess my writing as such. For one thing is certain, in addition to both taxation and death: we live amid the ubiquity of technology.

Hans Jonas (1903–1993) refers to technology as the "focal fact" of the present age.[1] Our present age is one in which beliefs in or of God might remain an option, as Charles Taylor has argued in *A Secular Age*, but encounter with various technologies is not. It is, at very least, an age in which it is disproportionately difficult to remain a Luddite. Technology pervades "almost everything vital to [our] existence—material, mental, and spiritual."[2] As such, we are a technological civilization. It might be, then, that the ubiquity of technology has formed me so completely to follow particular means that I am no longer free to be creative.

I will leave it to you, the reader, to determine which assessment is correct for the start of this volume. In what

1. Hans Jonas, "Towards a Philosophy of Technology," *Hastings Center Report* (February 1979): 34.
2. Jonas, "Towards a Philosophy of Technology," 34.

follows I aim to lead you through an analysis of our techno-logical age and the power(s) we think we possess—powers we often wonder where and how to deploy, or powers we wonder whether ought to be deployed at all.

We must wrestle with the question of power in our present age. Not only do we think we possess power in various forms, but also we are becoming increasingly aware about how much power is available. One needs only to consider the atomic powers wrought from the theoretical and physical sciences of the last centuries and determined necessary by the industries of energy and of war. We have long thought these powers were harnessed, but, with renewed global-political unrest and dilapidating infrastructure, they threaten once again both ecology and security. Consider too the powers that reify the strata of geology and liberate gaseous energy reserves from the bowels of the earth through hydraulic fracturing, risking the destabilization of faults and contaminating groundwater.

In addition to such powers implemented to harness and release energies and to control natural resources, we have over the last several decades observed increased knowledge and the development of powers to create and to recreate biological life and to remediate the deleterious effects of aging, dysfunction, and disease. We do this through advances emerging from genetic, epigenetic, and genomic research and their complementary biotechnologies and intelligent algorithms. We also face the inevitable human experiment to transplant a viable body from a vegeta-tive donor, attaching it to the head of another person whose body is otherwise terminally ill—a potentiality made possible by advances in chemical, neurological, and medical-surgical sciences. These powers and advances demonstrate the promise and peril of modern scientific and technological progress, both fostering the potential of extreme longevity and revealing the potentiality for dystopic futures.

With such examples one might be able to understand, in our technologically enhanced context, just how much power humanity has amassed and is pursuing. Many more examples could be introduced, ranging from the powers that emerged through the earliest mass-printing presses and steam engines through to the powers of nanotechnologies and brain-chip interfaces. One might also extend the imagination beyond mere machinery, pointing toward techniques incumbent to politics or perhaps writing (as I have suggested above). Regardless of the examples, power is what is most interesting.

Such power is interesting because, as Emmanuel G. Mesthene (1921–1990) suggests, the acquisition of power is what is *new* in our present age. He says that we are among the first "who can aspire to be free of the tyranny of physical nature" that has haunted humanity from the beginning.[3] Power, in

3. Emmanuel G. Mesthene, "Technology and Wisdom," in *Technology and Social Change*, ed. Emmanuel G. Mesthene (Indianapolis: Bobbs-Merrill, 1967), 57–62. French historian of philosophy Rémi Brague has similarly observed such aspiration and the actualization of such freedom. However, unlike Mesthene, Brague laments that, in modernity, humanity has conquered nature, but at a cost. Brague suggests that humanity, now a mere object of nature and of self-creation, is at risk of self-destruction. That is, as introduced in his preface, in modernity, while "knowledge of man freed itself from nature and from the divine," refusal "to derive its existence and legitimacy from any

this instance, might concern the capacities to change our physical environment. But power, for Mesthene, offers us more than the capacity to shape landscape and to construct built environments.[4] It includes the aspirations to amend our social and cultural milieu, to change the experiences and expressions of human beings (and being human). Such aspirations to change nature, including human nature, correspond well with what technology was for Mesthene: *an organization of knowledge for the purpose of accomplishing practical aims and achievements.*

Technology, as such, is fashioned after the modern *project*, which Rémi Brague suggests is pursued by our decision or desire. A project, in the modern sense, is that which "*we decide to undertake*, whereas a task is entrusted to us by some higher power: nature in pagan style, or God in biblical style."[5] Mesthene is suggesting, therefore, by his definition, that technology frees humanity *from* task obligations in pursuit of the project *for* our desires. Technology, then, might be considered as the *power to do* as intended.

place other than itself" risks great peril. See Brague, *The Kingdom of Man: Genesis and Failure of the Modern Project*, trans. Paul Seaton (Notre Dame: University of Notre Dame Press, 2018), xiii. The following will second such analysis.

4. Emmanuel Mesthene, *Technological Change: Its Impact on Man and Society* (New York: New American Library, 1970).
5. Rémi Brague, *Curing Mad Truths: Medieval Wisdom for the Modern Age* (Notre Dame: University of Notre Dame Press, 2019), 4 (emphasis added). See also Brague, *Kingdom of Man*, 2–5.

Yet to do as anyone might intend reflects a particular limitation in the human endeavor to pursue new knowledge-as-power. The current digital expressions of our technological age have introduced an *intelligent* civilization that takes advantage of artificial neural networks and machine-learning algorithms—to manage everything from medical diagnostics to targeted propaganda campaigns. The practical aims and achievements of our technological age, therefore, are increasingly conditioned by the forecasting of outcomes as large swaths of data are collated, processed, and analyzed. The organization of knowledge into patterns of information incumbent to the flow of data is prioritized, while decision-making models that adjust our aims and calculate the feasibility of achievements are valued. As such, intelligent technology might be thought as *the organization of information for the prediction and pursuit of practical outcomes and achievements*—a slight alteration to Mesthene's definition above. However, while such power is incumbent in the digital hypostases of our technological civilization, it remains restricted to those algorithms that can manage the massive data load. It is restricted because human beings are not able to process such data through traditional rationality, agency, and technique. Technology, as such, is *learning* to go "where no human has gone before—and where no human can follow."[6]

The question remains: Is Mesthene's definition, or the intelligent analogue, of technology suitable? Put differently,

6. Yuval Noah Harari, *Homo Deus: A Brief History of Tomorrow* (London: Vintage, 2016), 458.

how ought we to understand the essence of technology? It is an important question that must precede questions that aim to evaluate the pursuit of power by particular means or to challenge the promises (or probability) of digital forecasts. This question will allow us to discern the essential nature of technology.

Defining Technology

What is technology? The answer for what might seem a simple question is actually quite difficult to establish. Indeed, a great many have labored to delimit and to define technology. Consider George Parkin Grant (1918–1988), educated (in theology) at Oxford and regarded as one of Canada's foremost philosophers and public intellectuals. He sought on several occasions to examine the essential nature of technology. His writings on the subject were among the first in my academic formation to illuminate a counternarrative to the hegemony of modern values and progress. His doctoral dissertation, for example, which was a study of Scottish theologian John Oman's (1860–1939) understanding of nature and supernature, offers a glimpse into Grant's early thinking on the subject.

For Oman, one's experience of nature is to be the foundation for understanding nature rightly. But *nature* refers to the unsullied environment, not yet altered by human activity. Our experience and understanding, our perception, of nature, as nature is in itself, is becoming increasingly difficult to encounter. As Grant assesses, Oman feared that industrialism would deprive us all of "the vision of nature in any terms save that of the tourist resort."[7] This image of the tourist experience of nature, now sullied, is echoed by Martin Heidegger: "The Rhine is still a river in the landscape, is it not? Perhaps. But how? In no other way than as an object on call for inspection by a tour group ordered there by the vacation industry."[8]

In the end, nature becomes mere fodder for human usage. Such usage thus reorients one's perception of nature, demanding that one learns to see it as a mere image of the artifacts of industrial potential and power. As Oman illustrated for Grant: once we have discovered the industrial usage in a solid piece of wood, that is, its potential to be a lever for mechanical advantage, everything else about the wood recedes from view. The only thing we learn to see is its abstracted material and the mechanical properties that make it an ideal object to be used as a lever. The rigidity and strength of the wood occlude our original experience of a grand old oak that stands before us among a legion of mature trees in a virgin forest. Instead, such a tree, among the many measured out and numbered in a cut block, becomes interpreted as mere logs and planks to be hewn down by sawyers and crafted into usable objects by industrial logging companies and the like.

7. George Grant, "The Concept of Nature and Supernature in the Theology of John Oman, DPhil Thesis, Oxford 1950," in *Collected Works of George Grant*, vol. 1, *(1933-1950)*, ed. Arthur Davis and Peter C. Emberley (Toronto: Toronto University Press, 2000), 167–420 (239).
8. Martin Heidegger, *The Question Concerning Technology and Other Essays*, trans. William Lovitt (New York: Harper & Row, 1977), 16.

Oman's concern about our changing perceptions points in the direction of our modern world, which Grant later characterized as technological—a civilization conditioned to use, control, and manipulate nature: "Men proud of their ability to control nature, equated knowledge of nature with control of it. Philosophers of this period conceived nature from inference based on the ability to control it by explanations."[9] From these early studies and throughout his career, Grant gave attention to the study of *technology*, a word he used as an expression of what the modern world was all about—"that secular [modern] civilization is committed to human autonomy without God, and to science, technology, and industry guided only by human purposes."[10]

Of course, as Grant goes on to articulate in his later writings, when considering human purposes in the technological age, one is not considering teleology as in classical philosophy (e.g., Aristotelian intrinsic goods), but rather the monolithic reality of the technological society—namely, mastery.[11] Such mastery is concerned principally with the liberation of the individual from nature and the human condition, a condition marked by toil, fragility, and finitude.

While Grant's understanding of *technology* as a word that describes our modern world has significantly affected my

9. Grant, "Concept of Nature," 238.
10. Arthur Davis, "Editors' Introduction [to 'The Concept of Nature and Supernature in the Theology of John Oman, DPhil Thesis, Oxford 1950']," in Grant, *Collected Works of George Grant*, vol. 1, 157–66 (160).
11. Henry Roper, "Introduction to *Technology and Empire*," in *Collected Works of George Grant*, vol. 3, *(1960-1969)*, ed. Arthur Davis and Henry Roper (Toronto: Toronto University Press, 2005), 473–79 (477).

thinking, his is not the only study attempting to delimit the meaning of technology. Others have also offered critical insight. Yet it is important to note that *technology* is not the only word to consider in this area. *Technique* is also introduced. Complicating matters, these two terms are often confused and confusing. Further, I tend to use the terms with relative imprecision—as might already be clear above—and conventions for usage of the terms tend to be different depending on geography, that is, there is a European preference for *technique* and a North American preference for *technology*.

Exploring and making sense of the oddity of the terms helps us examine the essential nature of things, specifically the essential nature of the technological society—and keeps us from falling into the trappings of uncritical optimism, biased pessimism, or willful ignorance when considering the significance of technology.[12] For many, the parallel meaning of these terms ought to include the means of projects performed or procedures constructed that, with order and precision, regulation and control, expect to reproduce a particular means or manufacture a particular commodity. Consider further Gabriel Marcel, a French philosopher and playwright who was concerned that the conditions of our modern world created by the spirit of technology might inhibit the flourishing of human persons.[13] He defines *tech-*

12. Mesthene, *Technological Change*, 16–20.
13. For a good discussion of Marcel and technology, see Bernard A. Gendreau, "The Cautionary Ontological Approach to Technology of Gabriel Marcel," paper presented at the Twentieth World Congress of Philosophy (Boston, August 10–15, 1998).

nique as "a group of procedures, methodologically elaborated, and consequently capable of being taught and reproduced, and when these procedures are put into operation they assure the achievement of some definite concrete purpose."[14] His definition parallels that of Mesthene, which focuses on the organization of knowledge for practical purposes. Order, procedure, and reproducibility toward achieving a particular aim are common traits in the respective definitions. Yet Marcel continues by suggesting that a technique is something that we might acquire, learn, or possess by habit, thereafter warning, "If a man can become the slave of his habits, it is equally probable that he can become prisoner of his techniques." Such a warning will be explored later in further detail, but it does raise here a necessary hazard for definitions that have presented technology positively without the incumbent problem of mastery: Who or what is being mastered?

Warnings notwithstanding, though set in the background for now, let us continue to illuminate the (possible) meaning of technology, turning again to Grant's "Thinking about Technology." In this important essay, Grant labors to examine the meaning of technology, preferring the North American iteration, which brings to mind "the whole apparatus of instruments made by man and placed at the disposal of man for his choices and purposes."[15] We might see here

14. Marcel, *Man against Mass Society*, 62.
15. George Grant, "Thinking about Technology," in *Technology and Justice*, in *Collected Works of George Grant*, vol. 4, *(1970-1988)*, ed. Arthur Davis and Henry Roper (Toronto: Toronto University Press, 2009), 589–606 (595).

a parallel with Mesthene's definition above. Specifically, in each of the definitions introduced thus far, there is a particular rationality that delimits the meaning of technique/ technology. This rationality is one in which reified nature, including human nature, is studied, ordered, and ultimately controlled—all for the purpose of acquiring particular powers or attaining particular commodities through the apparatus possessed or practiced.[16]

Now a few points can become clearer. First, the definitions thus far presented position human will over technology, which is to be used for our service—for our benefit. Technology is advanced so as to grasp hold of the aims pursued by humanity. Second, technology represents a schema or strata of ordinal practices, parts, or procedures that, by their construction, determine the ends that are sought. That is to say, the apparatus introduced by a given technology provides the means for accomplishing the desired aim. For example, the automobile provided the means for speedy transportation, replacing horse-drawn carriages or other rudimentary methods of travel, to realize transportation aims for both human beings and economic commodities. Of course, with the high rate of speed and less-than-practiced operators, collisions, injuries, and deaths are consequent to the introduction of the automobile. This problem, of course, has sparked the active pursuit of alternative models of travel, including public transportation and,

16. For further discussion about such rationality, see Andrew Feenberg, *Between Reason and Experience: Essays in Technology and Modernity* (Cambridge, MA: MIT Press, 2010), 157–218.

recently, autonomous carriage. Intelligent autonomous vehicles, therefore, not only enable speedy mobility but also improve the efficiency and safety of motorized travel. As such, the apparatus of a given technology guarantees that the commodity will be produced with an efficiency of form and a determination that delimits the use of said technology. Unfortunately, the determining of the technology to produce or to procure the commodity for which it was crafted does challenge the creative agency introduced in the first observation, technology is for our benefit. Take note, therefore, that the second observation, technology determines the ends that are sought, returns us to the counsel offered by Marcel above; specifically, that we must consider who or what is in control.

Such considerations are taken up by a preeminent figure in the critical philosophy of technology, Jacques Ellul (1912–1994). Writing from the 1930s through the 1990s, including his *La Technique: L'enjeu du siècle* (which can be translated as "Technique: The stake of the century," published in English as *The Technological Society*) and *Propagandes* (*Propaganda*), Ellul identified many of the questions and concerns that the increasing powers of technology, in its modern iteration, have raised.[17] He contends that technology

---

17. George Grant regarded these two book as essential reading for all who wish to best understand present life caught up in the dynamo of our technological societies. See George Grant, "Review of *The Technological Society*, by Jacques Ellul," in *Collected Works of George Grant*, vol. 3, 413–18 (412). For Grant, Ellul was not only a notable source but also the catalyst that drew Grant toward the writings of Martin Heidegger, whose influence on Grant is significant as he wrestles to understand

ought to be understood as a constraining, if not overwhelming and ruthless, force that is beyond human control, transforming everything into its image, including human beings. So, in a manner comparable to Jonas above, Ellul observes that technology is decisive in understanding our present age.[18]

Ellul's observations, however, were fashioned with disquieted lament. His dirge: human beings "now live in conditions that are less than human."[19] These conditions are the outcome of technique. That is, for Ellul, the unifying force of technology determines human life accordingly. As such, to understand technology, one must become aware of its determinative, mechanical work: areas of life once subject to either necessity or fate are now susceptible to intervention and various manners of control by the exercise of human will and industry embodied in the machine.

Such intervention is the technological interruption necessitated by the emergence of preceding technological advances. Yet Ellul regarded the technological interruption as more than a mere nuisance. In interrupting human life as it has done, technology shows itself to behave as a clandestine tyrant that absorbs all in its path into a great totalitarian, homogenous whole,[20] putting to work those it seeks to

the essential nature of technology. Heidegger's questioning of technology will be discussed below.

18. Jacques Ellul, *Perspectives on Our Age*, ed. William H. Vanderburg, trans. Joachim Neugroschel (New York: Seabury, 1981), 32.

19. Jacques Ellul, *The Technological Society*, trans. John Wilkinson (New York: Vintage Books, 1964), 4.

20. See, for example, Jacques Ellul's discussions about *the autonomy of*

dominate. An appropriate, albeit somewhat dated, cultural image may be offered in television's *Star Trek: The Next Generation* (1987–1994), which personified the tyranny of technology in the form of the Borg, an alien chimera of biology and technology that assimilated all to work as one for "the Collective," contra organisms, and who warned that resistance was futile. The tyranny of technology is now portrayed in various vignettes of the British anthology *Black Mirror* (Channel 4, 2011–2014; Netflix, 2014–present), for example, with depictions of oppressive drones, dehumanizing rating/ranking applications, and technologically mediated fears that compel violence and contort human behavior. Resistance remains futile.

Concerned about such tyranny, Ellul was quick to point toward cautionary notes rather than to develop an apologetic for technology. While technology is a power that promises to give liberation, strength, facility, simplification, and enrichment, it fails to live up to the promise. This is not to suggest technology does not do what it sets out to do. Rather, it accomplishes its aims most effectively. The problem is that under its easily won rule, the very social structures of human life change—they become determined by technique.[21] Humanity, in the technological society, is thus determined to be increasingly passive, diminished to act only when called on by political instruction or by the demands of technology (often one and the same; i.e.,

technique or his discussion regarding *the totalitarian state* in *Technological Society*, 133–47, 284–91.

21. Jacques Ellul, *Propaganda: The Formation of Men's Attitudes*, trans. Konrad Kellen and Jean Lerner (New York: Vintage Books, 1973), 252–53.

consider the mechanics of biomedical ethical legislation where technological demands become political imperatives)—but never to act as a creative individual, only as a mere mechanism in the systems of progress and power.[22] With the popular brief history of tomorrow sketched by Yuval Noah Harari, our value as a cog in the proverbial machine might also be usurped by digital technologies. Such technologies do illuminate particular limitations by taking advantage of the tsunami wave of information in the data stream. Such a wave overwhelms our rational competencies by the sheer volume and rate of information transfer. Yet algorithms can manage and process such data with efficient ease. And so it seems humans are sent down a path to merely listen to and abide the commands of the algorithms.[23] Ellul thus laments that, under the weight and rule of technological tyranny, a society cannot be free (or strong, or competent, or otherwise); it can only be efficient. The diminution of society, of the particularity of societies, is what is at stake for Ellul.

Similar concerns can be seen in the work of Lewis Mumford (1895–1990), who was concerned that a transition from tool using to machine serving would capture human purpose and put it to work toward achieving the technological order of being, the remaking of all things in the image of the machine. Mumford, however, gives us pause before yielding to biased pessimism, reminding us, "Tool technics is but a

22. Ellul, *Propaganda*, 147–60.
23. Harari, *Homo Deus*, 428–62.

fragment of biotechnics: man's total equipment for life."[24]
For Mumford, every technology is but an extension of the
body, and he understands biotechnics accordingly:

> Through man's overdeveloped and incessantly active brain, he
> had more mental energy to tap than he needed for survival at
> a purely animal level; and he was accordingly under the neces-
> sity of canalizing that energy, not just into food-getting and
> reproduction, but into modes of living that would convert this
> energy more directly and constructively into appropriate cul-
> tural—that is, symbolic—forms. Cultural work, by necessity,
> took precedence over manual work; this involved far more
> than the discipline of hand, muscle, and eye in making and
> using tools. It likewise demanded a control of all man's bio-
> logical functions, including his bodily organs, his emotions,
> his sexual activities, his dreams. Even the hand was no mere
> horny work-tool: it stroked a lover's body, held a baby close to
> the breast, made significant gestures, or expressed in ordered
> dance and shared ritual some otherwise inexpressible senti-
> ment about life or death, a remembered past or an anxious
> future.[25]

For Mumford, humanity, in its early forms, survived with
the tools of most creatures, that is, teeth, hands, feet, and
the like. Such tools gave these persons the time to craft
extrabodily tools that eventually enriched the technology

---

24. Lewis Mumford, "Technics and the Nature of Man," *Technology and
    Culture* 7, no. 3 (1966): 307. In an updated iteration of Mumford's essay,
    he clarifies further: "Tool technics and our derivative machine tech-
    nics are but specialized fragments of biotechnics: and by biotech-
    nics one means man's total equipment for living." See *Philosophy and
    Technology: Readings in the Philosophical Problems of Technology*, ed. Carl
    Mitcham and Robert Mackey (New York: Free Press, 1983), 77–85 (79).
25. Mumford, "Technics and the Nature of Man," 306–7.

they shared with beasts while also benefiting their way(s) of living. The bodily correlates of our technologies are best exemplified in simple levers and various mechanics that build and carve, burrow and heave. Yet Mumford's image here is less obvious in the present iteration of the technological age, where zeros and ones, qubits and algorithms, often code the ways of technique.

Mumford's reflection reminds us that not all are entirely morose regarding technology. The concerns raised are valid and duly noted even by apologists of technology. Yet responding to the cautions and concerns, some reply predictably as those marching to order inside the omnipresent dynamo of the technological society:

> O Wonder!
> How many goodly creatures are there here!
> How beauteous mankind is! O brave new world!
> That has such people in it![26]

"O brave new world," where the technological fix is presented as the solution to those challenges that perturb humanity.[27] In Aldous Huxley's (1894–1963) important novel *Brave New World*, John the Savage quotes this verse from Shakespeare's *The Tempest* several times. "O wonder! . . . O brave new world!" reflects John in his initial amazement

---

26. Aldous Huxley, *Brave New World* (London: Lythway, 1932), 209; see also William Shakespeare's *The Tempest* (London: Hutchinson, 1985), 62.
27. Although not all agree with such presentations of the technological fix. See, for example, Max Black, "Nothing New," in *Ethics in an Age of Pervasive Technology*, ed. Melvin Kranzberg (Boulder, CO: Westview, 1980), 26–27.

of the state of things in the world outside the Reservation, where he was raised. However, as John continues to repeat this verse throughout Huxley's novel, his wonder at the brave new world changes—first corresponding to his expression of amazement but altering to mocking derision and ultimately to a poetic exclamation of protest.

One might consider Mesthene's position regarding technology to be similar to John's first glance: the panoply of problems facing humanity is to be remedied by the continuing advance of human intelligence, ingenuity, and industry. Such industry is not reducible to mechanical innovation but works through the adoption of technique in moral and political spheres: "Technological innovation therefore leads ultimately to a need for social and political innovation if its benefits are to be fully realized and its negative effects kept to a minimum."[28] This claim actually helps us to further understand the terms we are attempting to define.

This is because philosophers such as George Grant, Jacques Ellul, and Gabriel Marcel, among others, expose us to the breadth of technology in our present society, expanding its semantics and determining impact across a wide range. It is important, therefore, to take notice, in these attempts to delimit and to define technology, that we are not being introduced to mere machines. That is to say, technology is not intended to simply connote the various ways that cogs agitate and reel to pull levers or to push debris—although machines such as the Dragline excavators, oil derricks, and combine harvesters that dot the horizon of the southeastern

28. Mesthene, *Technological Change*, viii.

Saskatchewan prairie where I was raised are indeed technologies. No. Rather, technology, as Grant made clear, is "the ontology of our age"; it is the way the world is or has become.[29]

As such, rather than adopting either *technology* or *technique*, I will prefer the term *techno-ontology*. The *idea* of techno-ontology—technology as not merely a concept or construction but a way of seeing or a determining of our way of seeing the world—can therefore include a compendium of industrial, political, economic, and moral machinery that instrumentalizes knowing for the purposes of doing, and bureaucratizes both the control and the management of persons surveyed by the panoptic gaze and corresponding judgment of technique. It is techno-ontology that concerns many of the interlocutors I've relied upon thus far. Techno-ontology, and its clandestine tyranny to make everything into an image of efficient form, should stir not only concern but also protest.

Why protest? One might ask.

"Let us *understand*, and on the basis of our common understanding, *protest*." Ursula Franklin (1921–2016), in her 1989 Massey Lectures, although positive that "redemptive technologies" can be used to shape new practices of working and living together, concluded her original lectures while reciting the phrase attributed to the British peace movement, which protested the placement of missiles on home soil.[30]

29. Grant, "Thinking about Technology," 605.
30. Ursula Franklin, *The Real World of Technology*, CBC Massey Lecture Series (Montreal: CBC Enterprise, 1990), 130; rev. ed. (Toronto: House of Anansi, 1999), 133. The Massey Lectures, inaugurated in 1961 with

Just as those of the peace movement called forth protest from fellow British citizens, Franklin challenged listeners to protest and to survive technology (or techno-ontology, as I prefer) "until there is *change* in the structures and practices of the real world of technology, for only then can we hope to survive as a community." She concluded with a final clarion call: "If such basic change cannot be accomplished, the house that technology built will be nothing more than an unlivable techno-dump."

Such a call to protest might come a bit early in this volume. But with Marcel's warning above, and now Franklin's tempered lament, it is also becoming clear that in discussing techno-ontology and the powers that correspond, we are discussing no small matter. Rather, we are discussing *everything*.

Questioning *Everything*

Many consider *The Question Concerning Technology* (*Die Frage nach der Technik*) a seminal work on technology.[31] German

economist Barbara Mary Ward (1914–1981), are an annual lecture series on cultural, political, or philosophical themes by prominent intellectuals. The series was created to honor Vincent Massey (1887–1967), the eighteenth governor general of Canada, and is delivered across five public lectures, which are also published for radio (i.e., CBC's *Ideas* broadcast) and for print (House of Anansi Press).

31. Let me be clear: the aim of my engagement with Heidegger is not to enter into the fray of the narrower scholarly debate regarding Heidegger's philosophy. Even less is it to exact a position on Heidegger's critique of technology as being either a discerning break from Nazism or an apology for a past that celebrates the mythical connections of

philosopher Martin Heidegger (1889–1976) joins the likes of Mumford in sharing the historical period emerging from the Second World War. For such thinkers, the crisis of civilization is one where the machine dominates and where the promises of modernity have proven to be perilous. Yet Heidegger's critique of technology does not share the underlying optimism of Mumford's work.

Heidegger's *Question Concerning Technology* was published in 1954. An original manuscript was written five years previous for the Bremen Lectures. *The Question Concerning Technology* was a revision of the second part of the four-part lecture series,[32] which was the first public lecture Heidegger gave after the war. For Heidegger, World War II was a moment in world history that revealed the end of modernity; great achievements of modern will, reason, and technique gave way to both great dehumanization and absolute destruction. *The Question Concerning Technology* became his treatise on what technology *is* and how humanity might correspond to it. The aim is introduced in the opening paragraph as such: "We shall be questioning *technology*, and in so doing we would like to prepare a free relationship to it. The rela-

German rootedness. The aim is to reflect on the particular grammar Heidegger has used in discussing technology, which has influenced so many—including George Grant, among others—and gives us content to think further about technology.

32. The four-part lecture series has been translated and published in *Bremen and Freiburg Lectures: Insight into That Which Is and Basic Principles of Thinking*, Studies in Continental Thought, trans. Andrew J. Mitchell (Bloomington: Indiana University Press, 2012).

tionship will be free if it opens our human existence to the essence of technology."[33]

The questioning is done not to raise concern about the existence of technology per se. Rather, the questioning probes the corners and contours of our relationship to technology. Heidegger writes accordingly: "Thus we shall never experience our relationship to the essence of technology so long as we merely conceive and push forward the technological, put up with it, or evade it. Everywhere we remain unfree and chained to technology, whether we passionately affirm or deny it."[34]

Therefore, in his attempt to discern the essence of technology, Heidegger begins with the correct understanding of *Technik*. Specifically, Heidegger notes two answers often offered: first, technology is a means to an end; second, technology is a human activity.[35] Both responses are instrumental and anthropological, and seemingly impossible to deny. They therefore conceive and push forward the technological without further questioning. They conceal the essential nature as they *re-present* the conventional understanding.

Indeed, conventional understanding is difficult to deny. Consider, for example, scissors. They are a simple device that provides the efficient and valuable means of cutting various materials, from paper to wire, sheer curtains to sheet metal. Scissors fix the edges of two sharpened blades to a pivot, creating a simple machine—a class-one lever. In

33. Heidegger, *Question Concerning Technology*, 3.
34. Heidegger, *Question Concerning Technology*, 4.
35. Heidegger, *Question Concerning Technology*, 4.

this way, scissors provide the means for applying sheer force to materials for the end aim of predictably cutting materials. These tools correspond to the traditional "in order to" of technologies that might be reflected in the writings of Aristotle or other classical thinkers.

Yet, while this tool suits the *correct*, that is, *conventional*, definitions of technology above, such definitions (or the tools used to validate them) do not reveal the essence of technology. They fail to capture what technology is ontologically. Various artifacts of technology are made and implemented by human agents whose aim is to gain mastery over the products of their use; the will to such mastery becomes increasingly urgent as the powers wrought from the advance of technology threaten to become unwieldy. The instrumental and anthropological definitions are therefore unsatisfactory. That is, to repeat myself, such definitions occlude rather than disclose the essential nature of technology.

Scissors are designed for the human agent to organize the human force to wield the lever against the material being formed by the cutting exercise. One cannot deny that the scissor tool is a fitting example of a technology as defined by the convention above. Yet neither the scissors nor its implementation against the raw material it aims to shape helps us to understand the essence of technology. These merely reinforce conventional understanding, which is at once prima facie (conditional) rather than essential understanding.

If the conventional definition is not sufficient, what is technology?

Heidegger probes this question again and again throughout his treatise. To be sure, Heidegger is confident that technology is not a new phenomenon. He is clear that technology and the imposition of human will to take hold of and to master nature, to give shape to nature, including human nature (by habits of virtue, for example), have been pursued in the West for centuries, dating back as early as the ancient Greeks, if not further.

Human beings, he argues, are creative by nature and thus committed to *world making* through various modalities, ranging from language to the making and implementation of tools to *bring forth* or to reveal the human world. For Heidegger, this is what is meant by the Greek verb *poiēsis*—to make or to transform the world. Human beings, therefore, have been committed to the decisive actions of world making and revealing the essential nature of the relationship between nature and humanity.

However, a question must follow: If technology, as *poiēsis*, has always been in relation to human creative agency, to making, what is different in a modern context? What stirred Heidegger to continue probing the question of technology?

The answer might rest in Heidegger's observation that modern technology *enframes*.[36] "Enframing" (*Gestell*) is novel to the present age and in contradistinction to the long labor of becoming ready to live in the world.[37] Enframing is the way we are determined to *see* the world, each other, and ourselves. Put differently, enframing concerns the determi-

36. Heidegger, *Question Concerning Technology*, 20.
37. Martin Heidegger, "Overcoming Metaphysics," in *The End of Philosophy*, trans. Joan Stambaugh (Chicago: University of Chicago Press, 2003), 84–110 (109).

native meaning making of technology that sees in nature, including human nature, the raw material to be used for something. When such raw material is proven to be an object without use, it is discarded or disposed of:

> Imagine a garden with a hundred kinds of trees, a thousand kinds of flowers, a hundred kinds of fruit and vegetables. Supposed, then, that the gardener of this garden knew no other distinction than between edible and inedible, nine-tenths of this garden would be useless to him. He would pull up the most enchanting flowers and hew down the noblest trees and even regard them with a loathing and envious eye.[38]

In being used, objects of nature, inert until acted on, become something—but only in relation to their instrumental usage, determined by calculable plans and measures. Therefore, the material object, including human material, becomes enframed by purpose, which is not natural but commodified. Here we might be reminded of Mesthene's belief that technology can be defined as an organization of knowledge for the purpose of accomplishing practical aims and achievements. However, Mesthene is not following Heidegger's analysis. Rather than enframing meaning, Mesthene believes technology is open to a range of possible effects.[39] Once again, Mesthene's wonder might reflect John the Sav-

38. Hermann Hesse, *Steppenwolf*, trans. Basil Creighton (London: Penguin Books, 1965), 75. Also see Brian Brock's *Christian Ethics in a Technological Age* (Grand Rapids: Eerdmans, 2010), 66–101. Brock uses this quote as an epigraph for his essay that considers the influence of Heidegger on Grant's understanding and critique of technology.
39. Emmanuel Mesthene, "The Role of Technology in Society," *Technology and Culture* 10, no. 4 (1969): 489–536.

age's initial expressions of amazement and awe—at the very least, Mesthene remains positive. For Heidegger, the essence of technology, unveiled by the horrors of the Second World War, is much more sinister.

The *essence* of technology in the modern world, which Heidegger sought to understand, is not technology itself. It is not located in the conventional definitions offered, that technology is a means to an end and a human activity. Rather, the essence of technology makes modern ingenuity and industry possible by revealing a world where everything is observed as a raw material awaiting meaning-making activity—waiting, standing at the ready, to be used for a purpose (or waiting with unremitting anxiety to be discarded as purposeless). Having observed this state of affairs, Heidegger laments:

> The unnoticeable law of the earth preserves the earth in the sufficiency of the emerging and perishing of all things in the allotted sphere of the possible which everything follows, and yet nothing knows. The birch tree never oversteps its possibility. The colony of bees dwells in its possibility. It is first the will which arranges itself everywhere in technology that devours the earth in the exhaustion and consumption and change of what is artificial. Technology drives the earth beyond the developed sphere of its possibility into such things which are no longer a possibility and are thus the impossible. The fact that technological plans and measures succeed a great deal in inventions and novelties, piling upon each other, by no means yields the proof that the conquests of technology even make the impossible possible.[40]

40. Heidegger, "Overcoming Metaphysics," 109.

Heidegger's lament might be joined also by those of the Frankfurt school, including Max Horkheimer (1895–1973) and Theodor Adorno (1903–1969). In exile from their homeland, demeaned by Nazi control, and living in the United States (although a refuge, not an ideal location), Horkheimer and Adorno criticized the Enlightenment predominance of technological rationalities that render everything an object of knowledge and fodder for domination.[41] Accordingly, as they comment in their treatise on schematism in *The Dialectic of Enlightenment*, "Everything—even the human individual, not to speak of the animal—is converted into a repeatable, replaceable process, into a mere example for the conceptual models of the system."[42] Such thinking compelled them to see fascism, not to mention Stalinism and consumer capitalism, as the climax of *enlightened* agency—political systems of domination cultivated by technological rationalities and the concomitant administration of false systems that proffer commodities but suffer authentic culture. Their concern was with the way such political systems have come to see everything, including everyone, as an object for use and ultimately disposable: "What men want to learn from nature is how to use it in order wholly to dominate it and other men. That is the only game."[43]

41. For accounts of Adorno's time in America, see Martin Jay, "Adorno in America," *New German Critique* 31 (1984): 157–82; Peter U. Hohendahl, "The Displaced Intellectual? Adorno's American Years Revisited," *New German Critique* 56 (1992): 76–100.
42. Max Horkheimer and Theodor W. Adorno, *The Dialectic of Enlightenment*, trans. John Cumming (New York: Continuum, 1996), 84.
43. Horkheimer and Adorno, *Dialectic of Enlightenment*, 4.

So, what is the essence of technology?

Technology is more than a mundane tool for human agency to pursue particular ends of mastery and control. Technology represents a posture that can be taught. It is a posture committed to a knowing that seeks to control all of nature, including human nature, in an attempt at instrumental meaning making. It is the way in which we have been trained to see everything in the world, including we in it—a collection of inert machines awaiting animation (or annihilation). Thus, by such revealing, by such training, the now-familiar maxim "knowledge is power" comes to mean the power to master the material universe by enframing it to form and function for a purpose imposed on raw material—and humanity has certainly demonstrated a profound capacity for mastery. Such mastery has been exercised by human agency committed to, and determined by, the forward campaign of technological progress. The challenge for humanity benefiting from such progress is that the imperative purpose proffered by technology to pursue such mastery and the outcomes thus far achieved make it quite difficult to criticize the essential nature and continued promise of technology. Yet criticism is warranted, perhaps even protest. Why? The issue has to do with power—power that can grasp the good ends pursued by will, as the hand of Adam that grasps hold the fruit of a tree.

Such rationality is exemplified in the Renaissance, with both René Descartes (1596–1650) and Francis Bacon (1561–1626) standing as principal representatives of the period. Descartes, for example, in his *Discourse on Method*, sees the promise of emerging knowledge from a utilitarian method in terms of resolving problems of labor, vitality, and aging.[44] The commodities such aims acquire justify the pursuit of scientific enquiry and technological innovation. Likewise, Bacon, and the above maxim often attributed to him, sees the scientific method as the mechanism that might give strength for dominating nature; it is where "human knowledge and human power, do really meet in one."[45] Various techniques that accompany modern knowing become the way said knowledge—that is, power—is put to work, shaping the elemental world to form and set toward resolving the problems of pain, and bolstering the benefits of pleasure. For Bacon, this is the end, or aim, of modern scientific endeavor. His *New Atlantis*, accordingly, imagines a society dedicated to the scientific methodology and the domination of nature. The rationality emerging from the Renaissance exemplifies a will to master, a will to power.

It was Heidegger who forewarned, "The will to mastery becomes all the more urgent the more technology threatens to slip from human control."[46] In the "age of exclusive power of power," being (*Dasein*), human existence, risks becoming conscripted, used up, and forgotten in the ongoing struggle

44. René Descartes, "Discourse on Method," in *The Philosophical Writings of Descartes*, trans. John Cottingham, Robert Stoothoff, and Dugald Murdoch (Cambridge: Cambridge University Press, 1985), 1:109–76.

45. Francis Bacon, "The Plan of Work," in *New Atlantis and the Great Instauration*, rev. ed., ed. Jerry Weinberger (Malden, MA: Wiley-Blackwell, 1989), 19–34 (32). See also Bacon's use of the Latin phrase "ipsa scientia potestas est" (knowledge itself is power), as written in his "Of Heresies," in *Meditationes Sacrae* (1597).

46. Heidegger, *Question Concerning Technology*, 5.

for mastery over that which is elemental.[47] The second chapter will explore this hazard in further detail, but it demands some explanation now: Heidegger is concerned that human beings risk becoming raw material awaiting meaning-making activity. Thus, he grieves:

> The consumption of all materials, including the raw material "man," for the unconditioned possibility of the production of everything is determined in a concealed way by the complete emptiness in which being, the materials of what is real, is suspended. This emptiness has to be filled up by the fullness of beings, especially when this emptiness can never be experienced as such, the only way to escape it is incessantly to arrange being in the constant possibility of being ordered as the form of guaranteeing aimless activity. Viewed in this way, technology is the organization of a lack, since it is related to the emptiness of Being contrary to its knowledge. Everywhere where there are not enough beings—and it is increasingly everywhere and always not enough for the will to will escalating itself—technology has to jump in, create a substitute, and consume the raw materials.[48]

Grant captures a similar concern, warning that human agency might be lost as one is captured by an endlessly reciprocating technological mechanism, that is, the dynamo where technological solutions are introduced, or rather demanded, "to meet the emergencies which technology has produced."[49] So, rather than meaningful creative agency, one is caught in the calculable machination of the will to

47. Heidegger, "Overcoming Metaphysics," 104.
48. Heidegger, "Overcoming Metaphysics," 105–6.
49. Grant, "Thinking about Technology," 593.

will, that is, technology. It is no wonder that Hans Jonas declared, as introduced above, that technology is the focal fact of modern life, touching everything that is vital for existence, calculating the earth, and subduing the particularity of being.

This focal fact of modern life, that is, technology, is more than a commonplace tool for human agency to pursue particular ends of mastery and control. Chip Walter regards such pursuit as pivotal in human evolution, granting us new possibilities regarding what we might be able to do with ourselves and each other.[50] Yet the very technology developed to bring the world, including the self and others, under the control of human will and energy threatens to radically reconstruct and possibly destroy human being, seizing power over against human control—and it might have done so already.

So, we must ask ourselves, following the questioning of Heidegger: Should one understand this threat as a warning or as an apt description of what is? Should one understand this as dubious folly or emerging fate?

Techno-Ontology as the Fate of the World

Technology is everything, the ontology of our age: If that is the case, then what might we expect? This is a question taken up by Grant in an interview by Gad Horowitz at Grant's

50. Chip Walter, *Thumbs, Toes, and Tears: And Other Traits That Make Us Human* (New York: Basic Books, 2006).

Ontario home in 1969. Here are the first two questions and responses at length:

HOROWITZ: What do you mean when you describe our society as a technological society?

GRANT: I mean that this is a society in which people think of the world around them as mere indifferent stuff which they are absolutely free to control any way they want through technology. I don't think of the technological society as something outside us, you know, like just a bunch of machines. It is a whole way of looking at the world, the basic way Western men experience their own existence in the world. Out of it comes large organizations, bureaucracies, machines, and the belief that all problems can be solved scientifically, in an immediate quantifiable way. The technological society is one in which men are bent on dominating and controlling human and non-human nature.

HOROWITZ: And out of this dominating, aggressive relationship with nature grows a situation in which human beings are prevented from existing truly as human beings. Their lives are shaped to conform to the requirements of technological progress. They thus become subordinated to their own technology. How do you mean this? In what ways can we see it? In what ways are we as human beings damaged by the technological relationship with nature?

GRANT: I think that fundamentally, we don't quite know what has happened to us. What I try to say in [Technology and Empire] is that we must try to think what it is to live in modern North America. We who have walked the streets of the great metropolis, and seen the giant wars of this century, and live in highly organized institutions which determine us more than we determine them, must feel the need not only to live but to know, to think our living—otherwise we are at the mercy of it.

And it seems to me at the moment that we are at the mercy of the technological machine we have built, and every time anything difficult happens, we add to the machine. We have more science to answer the difficulties that science itself has created. Now this predicament is too enormous in the history of the race to permit one to say: I'm against it, or I'm for it. The main thing, you know, in my life, is just to see what it is. Technology is the metaphysics of our age, you know, it is the way being appears to us, and certainly we're rushing into the future with no categories by which we can judge it.[51]

As one might notice, Grant was influenced by Heidegger's philosophy of technology, which introduced Grant to the homogenizing impact of technology: the essence of technology is that it "enframes" the world.[52] In this world, everything, including us human inhabitants, is "hypostasize[d] as technique."[53] Everything becomes indifferent stuff to be molded, manipulated, and made for use—only then might meaning be provisionally bestowed, until the substrate for doing is used up.

The aim is to acquire a particular modality of power that

---

51. George Grant and Gad Horowitz, "'Technology and Man': An interview of George Grant by Gad Horowitz," in Grant, *Collected Works of George Grant*, vol. 3, 595–602 (595–96). For Grant's *Technology and Empire*, see *Collected Works of George Grant*, vol. 3, 473–594.

52. Although influenced by the likes of Simone Weil, Leo Strauss, Jacques Ellul, and others, and by the late 1960s onward Friedrich Nietzsche and Martin Heidegger, Grant resourced his philosophical imagination regarding his reflections concerning modernity and technology. See Arthur Davis, "Introduction to Volume 3: 1960–1969," in Grant, *Collected Works of George Grant*, vol. 3, xvii–xxv (xxi).

53. George Grant, "Excerpts from Seminar Lectures on Heidegger, 1972–3 and 1978–9," in *Collected Works of George Grant*, vol. 4, 1019–35 (102).

asserts dominance and control over the objects awaiting meaning-making activity. Thus, all things, including human "things," are objectified, ordered, and put to process or to procedure (and, for those being replaced, put out to pasture). This describes the metaphysics of the modern world—it is how we have come to see the nature of things. Put differently, the impact of techno-ontology on our society is that it has schematized everything into categories for calculation, quantification, and use; and, as Grant suggested, it is by technological means that we approach every crisis we encounter, including the crisis of technology itself.[54] The result of this circular trap is that we struggle to see the essence of technology and fail to judge it rightly. Furthermore, we fail to ready ourselves for protest, *for we might be as technology has made us.*

54. One might consider, for example, the Anthropocene and the environmental and climate crises introduced by human impact, and accelerated by the output and waste of industrial feats once prized for progress but proving perilous, now thought to be retarded and possibly remedied by the advance and advantage of more technological (industrial, political, and moral) invention and intervention.

2

The Determining Potential
of Techno-Ontology

The first chapter sought to examine the meaning of technology and to introduce the crisis of this volume. However, I do not sketch out the crisis by particular dilemmas brought about by technological innovations and their usage. Such a picture would arbitrarily elevate one artifact of technology over another and, using a medical metaphor, become distracted by symptoms, rather than give due attention toward causes.

Nevertheless, I must concede, it might be easier to consider any one of these dilemmas as an important crisis ready for adjudication, and therefore worthy of attention. For example, one might consider data hacking and social media–enabled dissemination of disinformation. Alternatively, one might consider the biological and ecological uncertainties raised by the specter of gene-driven technologies, including the use of clustered regularly interspaced short palindromic repeats (CRISPR Cas9) to edit the genes of humans and/or other animals. One might also examine machine learning, and artificial intelligence and its impact on the future of work. Finally, one might study the visions of transhumanists and evaluate whether conceptions and experiences of human being, as we know of them now, are at risk of being irreversibly changed or extinguished by the introduction and adoption of technological enhancements.

Surely these examples highlight some of the technologies of interest or of moral and political significance at present. Yet this volume is not interested in these or other cases, as such. If it were, I would take up, as I alluded to in the prologue, the relevant questions incumbent to war and terror, and the technics of security and dominance that goad military aggression and lead to violence as the first response. Instead, we must continue the labor of discerning the content and contours of technology. We must do so both to see the crisis and to respond with and for all those persons who, wittingly or unwittingly, are caught up by it.

To this point, we have encountered several definitions of technology. Emmanuel Mesthene's definition has been the principal foil: knowledge put to work for acquiring particular commodities. Similarly, Gabriel Marcel considers technology as an operationalized pedagogy and practice that guarantees particular outcomes. Others saw with technology the constellation of means for achieving one's choices or purposes. Such definitions seem to correspond to the conventional definition of technology that Martin Heidegger was concerned concealed rather than revealed the essential nature of technology—it occluded rather than unfettered its meaning.

Hans Jonas and Jacques Ellul understand technology in terms of its ubiquity and totalizing impact on contemporary society. But Lewis Mumford sees technology as an extension of humans' readiness for attending to life. The range of reflection on technology offered by the various voices above, and others noted in the first chapter, extends from moderated optimism and cautious praise through to unencumbered pessimism. But it is George Grant's depiction of technology as an ontology that culminated in a reading of Heidegger and the enframing effects of technology—a determining that makes of nature, including human nature, the mere material that remains meaningless unless put to work toward some commodity that proffers power. Or, put differently, Russian philosopher Nicholas Berdyaev considers that the determining of human life is where persons are caught up by the organizing forces of rationalization, mechanization, bureaucratization, and materialization.[1] As such, technology, or my preferred term, *techno-ontology*, is a concern that our attention can be marshaled to see nature as reified and instrumental, rendering everything an object of knowledge and for the making of power for power. Meanwhile, all materials not suited for such means, including human

1. Berdyaev, "Spiritual Condition of the Modern World," 56–68.

"material," are determined as redundancies or waste. Technology's being, therefore, is a being with a singular determination: objectification for power.

The question of power shall be a focus of this chapter. It carries forward the concerns raised previously, sketching them again, but from a different perspective. The following will examine how we may have been so formed by the ontology of technology.

Modern Habits, Promising Power

We have gained much from the Galilean scientific legacy, which measures the world so as to master the world. Galileo Galilei (1564–1642), following after theories introduced by Nicolaus Copernicus (1473–1543), argued that nature was inherently coded by mathematics. The predictive calculations of Jacob Bernoulli (1655–1705) and the advent of probabilistic analysis of data, which Charles Darwin's (1809–82) demography capitalized on to predict the likelihood of genetic mutations, further demonstrated the power of numbers to explain the world, past, present, and future. In these ways the book of nature is to be read by the language of mathematics. Through such fundamental science, the reality behind natural phenomena might be known. Likewise, and perhaps with greater emphasis, physicist Max Tegmark, in *Our Mathematical Universe: My Quest for the Ultimate Nature of Reality*, argues that not only is nature to be read by mathematics, but it *is* mathematics.[2]

And so, as Tegmark has joked, Douglas Adams's (1952–2001) *answer* in the comedic science-fiction novel *The Hitchhiker's Guide to the Galaxy* actually follows the logic of the Galilean claim.[3] Mathematics, or the integer forty-two, specifically, might be the ultimate answer to the question of life, of everything. At very least, for Galileo, Tegmark, and others, such as Bertrand Russell (1872–1970), mathematics possesses both truth and beauty.[4]

Because the universe is a mathematical one, to be understood by the numbers, so to speak, Galileo advocated for a systematic study of nature through observation, measurement, and analytical attention to the events of nature so as to grasp hold of the hidden causes that give way to the expression of nature. The effectiveness of mathematics for explanatory power has been celebrated time and again.[5] We see renewed interest in such precision, for example, through the promises of genetic engineering and machine learning.

2. Max Tegmark, *Our Mathematical Universe: My Quest for the Ultimate Nature of Reality* (New York: Knopf, 2014).
3. For further reflections on science fiction and its influence in or on our technological age, see Michael S. Burdett, "Science Fiction and the Technological Imagination," in *Eschatology and the Technological Future* (New York: Routledge, 2014), 47–79.
4. Bertrand Russell, "The Study of Mathematics," in *Mysticism and Logic and Other Essays* (London: Allan & Unwin, 1918), 58–73. https://tinyurl.com/uz64mdy.
5. See, for example, Eugene Wigner, "The Unreasonable Effectiveness of Mathematics in the Natural Sciences," *Communications in Pure and Applied Mathematics* 13, no. 1 (1960): 1–14.

The aim, of course, is to acquire sufficient genomic data across a wide range of persons, heterogeneous in scope and diverse in disease, such that the data might be spun up, partitioned, and analyzed by increasingly efficient and effective machine interfaces and algorithmic predictions, to be put to use by correlative industries, creative developers, and competent health-care professionals.[6] The point is that such innovation can foster further innovation and intervention to persons struggling and desiring to live well. Living well, then, becomes delimited by the objectivity of numerical data points and predictions, and made probable by the advent of technological artifacts. Meanwhile, biopolitical and corporate-economic phenomena remain occluded by the technological promises to procure well-being against the backdrop of reality, including the actualities of frailty and finitude—that is, we remain unaware of the profits made by our complicity in consuming the products that technologies have determined we need.

Yet the causes of such frailty and finitude are algorithmically ordered. They become data no longer tied to "the order of myths, theogonies, or fabulations, [but] instead became *hypotheses* susceptible to corroboration or refutation by actual experiments,"[7] or disease-prediction modeling. The

---

6. Of course, while such predictive powers would be improved by much larger data sets, they would not be perfect: Hwasoon Kim, Alexander Gruenberg, Ana Vazquez, Stephen Hsu, and Gustavo De Los Campos, "Will Big Data Close the Missing Heritability Gap?," *Genetics* 207, no. 3 (2017): 1135–45.

7. Quentin Meillassoux, *After Finitude: An Essay on the Necessity of Contingency*, trans. Ray Brassier (London: Continuum, 2008), 114.

outcome of Galilean sciences, accordingly, is that the world, and we in it, can be described atomically, observing discrete characteristics or phenomena without connection or correlation to either sensible or teleological foundations. In this way, the world of Galileo, as with the one described also by Copernicus and Descartes, is "a world more indifferent than ever to human existence, and hence indifferent to whatever knowledge humanity might have of it. In this way, [modern] science carried within it the possibility of transforming every datum of our experience into a dia-chronic object—into a component of a world that gives itself to us as indifferent, in being what it is, to whether it is given or not."[8]

If the stuff of nature is indifferent, if it exists without an essential telos, a purposed *quidditas*,[9] then nature is merely matter. But basic sciences that labor to uncover and to merely describe indifferent matter are not sufficient in the modern period; rather, such sciences are not sufficient for those committed to a *Baconian* modernity. Matter must be made meaningful *in relation* to something else. The inert matter is without significance or meaning until it is put to use. Thus, the stuff of nature, including human nature, becomes seen as mere matter awaiting meaning-making

8. Meillassoux, *After Finitude*, 116.
9. A Latin term, meaning "whatness." That is, *quidditas* refers to the essence that which something is, i.e., the "treeness" of a rowan ash or a quaking aspen. Thomas Aquinas writes that *quidditas* is the nature or essence that exists in corporeal matter ("quidditas sive natura in materia corporali," *Summa Theologica* I.84.7).

agency—awaiting guidance toward production and the extrinsic *know-how* for motive change and usefulness.

So, nature, including our own nature, becomes delimited not by essence but by utility, not by form but by the possibility to grasp power over nature, to mold it to form in the modern Baconian sense, for the benefit of autonomy (self-making). Nature becomes the inert substance with which and by which we (inert substances too) take advantage over nature to form it and ourselves into the image of ideal order. To fail at cultivating such a relationship is to risk meaninglessness, to succumb to nihilism. The instrumental logic, therefore, becomes the device by which we might secure meaning—meaning-by-doing-shaping-making. Thus, the Galilean tradition of the sciences, further conditioned by Baconianism, has elaborated an epistemology that services, and possibly serves, the ontology of our age, technology.

The promise of power cultivated by technology, then, is a bulwark against pessimism and despair. In fact, the Baconian tradition, the progenitor of our technological age, offers us a meaning-making enterprise that incorporates a justificatory positive feedback loop: Baconianism promises power by knowing-making [technology] that emerges from the fodder of scientific discovery. Put differently, technology secures power, demonstrating the reliability of scientific epistemology that promises power.

"Mesmerized by the order, the precision, and, ultimately, what technology can provide us," we have learned to trust such promises for power.[10] In so doing, we have been

10. Burdett, *Eschatology and the Technological Future*, 60.

(re)ordered by a modern history that "sacralizes the world in new ways," as Bronislaw Szerszinski argues. In fact, for Szerszinski, as Philip Hefner summarizes, "It is not too much to say that science and technology express the ways we are religious today—science sketching the overarching order, technology focusing on how we ought to live; science assuming the status of 'new revelation' and technology becoming the religious way of life."[11]

Although there are many whose commitment to such a way of life is orthodox, there are some whose techno-fundamentalism best exemplifies such Baconian pursuits. One might consider, for example, those committed to the transhumanist declaration.[12] As David Pearce comments, reflecting the Baconian imagination in pursuit of a new Atlantis, "If we want to live in paradise, we will have to engineer it ourselves. If we want eternal life, then we'll need to rewrite our bug-ridden genetic code and become god-like. . . . Only hi-tech solutions can ever eradicate suffering from the world. Compassion alone is not enough."[13]

Confronting such fundamentalism, we might become aware that modern sciences and technologies can be and are being used to order nature accordingly, that is, to suit

11. Philip Hefner, "Religion and Science: Separateness or Co-inherence?," *Zygon*, 41, no. 4 (December 2006): 781–84 (781).
12. Doug Baily, Anders Sandberg, Gustavo Alves, Max More, Holger Wagner, et al., "Transhumanist Declaration," Humanity+, March 2009, https://tinyurl.com/v2vt4bz.
13. David Pearce, "Interview mit Nick Bostrom und David Pearce," *Cronopis* (December 2007), https://tinyurl.com/quyoppr.

the sacral reordering of the will to form.[14] We must, therefore, become aware of the modern *habitus* of our technological age, which has ushered in a radically immanent form of the sacred that trains one to see, in the agency of humanity governed by the reciprocal activity of the sciences and technologies, the means to meaning-making discovery—to discover the power *to become* masters and gods, in control over the stuff of nature.

I will explore this modern habitus further, studying the relationship of the sciences to technology. By exploring the sacralizing means of the sciences and technologies in the modern world, I hope that we might be able to better understand the crisis of an age where technology defines, delimits, and determines the nature of things. As the relationship unfolds, as helpful metaphors are introduced, our conclusion will lead us toward the principal problem of techno-ontology—its determining and dehumanizing tyranny.

The Pedagogy of Baconian Power

Nicholas Berdyaev speaks of the quest for power in his *The Fate of Man in the Modern World*. Yet Berdyaev is careful to position this fate as a theological concern in relation to the quest for power by a technological rationality that arose from the Renaissance through to modern anthropology: "In making himself God," Berdyaev accuses, "man has

---

14. Bronislaw Szerszinski, *Nature, Technology, and the Sacred* (Malden, MA: Blackwell, 2005), 172.

unmanned himself."[15] Accordingly, the world where we seek to control by measure is a world in which we forge a bestial inhumanity where no telos exists; it is replaced by an instrumental logic rationalizing the promise of power—perhaps thought of now as the totem we revere as sacred and around which society is gathered, directed, and defined.[16] Accordingly, Berdyaev writes: "Man desires power, power for himself, but this leads him to put power above self, above [fellow] man; it leads him to readiness to sacrifice his own humanity [as that of his fellows] for the sake of power."[17] Power in this way trains us to see the world, including both our fellows and ourselves, as machine parts or anticipatory data streams.

15. Nicholas Berdyaev, *The Fate of Man in the Modern World*, trans. Donald Lowrie (San Rafael, CA: Semantron, 2009), 29.
16. Although critical of Émile Durkheim's sociological positivism, Berdyaev thought Durkheim was correct concerning the sociological fact and derivation of religion. See Nicholas Berdyaev, *Filossofia svobodnogo dukkha* [Philosophy of free spirit] (Moscow: Respublika, 1994), 13–228. Accordingly, the observation might be apt: "In themselves, neither man nor nature is inherently sacred," Durkheim argues. Rather, he continues, "both acquire sacredness elsewhere. Beyond the human individual and the natural world, then, there must be some other reality in relation to which this species of delirium that every religion is, in some sense, takes on meaning and objective significance. In other words, beyond what has been called naturism and animism, there must be another more fundamental and more primitive cult." See Durkheim, *The Elementary Forms of the Religious Life*, trans. Karen E. Fields (New York: Free Press, 1995), 84–85. The more primitive cult, according to Durkheim, is *totemism*. Power wrought from knowing and embodied in technology might be the modern totem. It narrates and nurtures the ontology of our age.
17. Berdyaev, *Fate of Man*, 30.

Such fate raises concern about the quest for power incumbent to our technological age. For Berdyaev, the quest is idolatrous, exemplifying a solitary quest divorced from both God and fellow humanity. For others, the solitary quest exemplifies a Promethean hubris to unlock the mysteries of the cosmos so as to gain the powers of the gods, to be(come) as God.[18] This is a provocative indictment. Yet the indictment is of principal concern for Berdyaev, not only because of the sin of idolatry but also because he worries that such aims ready humanity for great loss.

But what might be lost?

As techno-ontology takes hold, humanity is so also conformed. The human potential for diverse creativity and difference is replaced by the functional certainty and homogeneity of technique. Human beings are subjected to such functional certainty and homogeneity, contributing further to their conformation: "Technical civilization demands that man shall fulfil one or another of his functions, but it does not want to reckon with man himself—it knows only his functions. This is not dissolving man in nature, but making him into a machine."[19]

Furthermore, such a functional approach to understanding human beings corresponds to the contemporary inclination to further reduce human persons to conduits for data

18. I will return to this image. The Greek imagery of Prometheus, the creator of humanity and the one who stands against Zeus in rebellion and retaliation, is important. In the modern sense, the imagery reflects the buffered state: we too labor against God (or the gods) in the name of freedom, i.e., self-making.
19. Berdyaev, *Fate of Man*, 33.

acquisition, targets for procuring information. As human limitations expose their functional incompetence to be(come) data-processing machines, relative to data-processing algorithms and artificial-intelligence technologies, their practical value will be diminished and proven redundant in the data-driven digital age of technology.

Such is the significant crisis of our age. Techno-ontology is a crisis for the image of humanity, who becomes a machine implemented into the schema of nature. Such an image is anathema to the image of humanity delimited by the *imago Dei*. Accordingly, as Berdyaev emphasizes: "Man cannot be the image either of [inert] nature or of the [useful] machine. Man is the image and likeness of God."[20] But the secularization of nature, including human nature, through the heterodox habitus of our technological age has reordered the respective images.[21] So, the former image of inert nature and useful machines becomes normative, while the latter image and likeness of God is made impotent or, at best, instrumentalized for the private sphere.

The crisis reflects the tendency of our technological age to objectify and to instrumentalize everything and everyone. Thus, we learn to observe nature as inert, as meaningless, until rendered in mechanistic terms—meaningful as parts in a system to be studied and directed to instrumental ends, or as information-become-data to be analyzed and commanded according to projections and probabilities. This is the reason

20. Berdyaev, *Fate of Man*, 34.
21. Szerszinski, *Nature, Technology, and the Sacred*, 3–27; Hefner, "Religion and Science," 781.

we might refer to technology as the ontology of our age or, as I prefer, use the neologism *techno-ontology*. In using this term, I am identifying particular problems that one must consider.

First is the problem of hubris or sin incumbent to the modern project. As stories of secularization are told, the sacred is being reordered by the secular. Porous life is being replaced or rearranged by the buffered life.[22] As the advance of scientific knowledge and corresponding technology continue to present tangible advantage against the limits and frailties of human life in nature, there is a retreat (or reorientation) of faith. So, as secularization narratives often conclude, through the advantage proffered by modern will, reason, and technique, we mere mortals have proven ourselves self-sufficient, solitary, and strong. We can exclaim, with Friedrich Nietzsche's (1844–1900) notorious madman: "God is dead! God remains dead! And we have killed him!"[23]

For many, such a death is ideal. Birthed of Renaissance anthropologies, it reflects, as the supposed pinnacle of human freedom, that we are now gods by our own making, not through deification but through deicide, not through participation with but pretension against God. However, for

22. Charles Taylor, "Buffered and Porous Selves," *The Immanent Frame* (blog), September 2, 2008, https://tinyurl.com/y2gzwddb. For a more robust treatment of these themes, see Charles Taylor, "The Bulwarks of Belief," in *A Secular Age* (Cambridge, MA: Harvard University Press, 2007), 25–89.

23. Friedrich Nietzsche, *The Gay Science*, trans. Josephine Nauckhoff and Adrian del Caro, ed. Barnard Williams (Cambridge: Cambridge University Press, 2001), 120.

others, such a death reflects Promethean hubris or Adamic sin. The problem relates to the idea that we alone by our own atomized agency can recognize evil and build the good life, the *summum bonum*. We can become masters of and over our fate.

At very least, such haughty efforts risk folly, unintended consequences, and tragedy. The excessive pride in human agency, to secure our desires by the administration of modern means, risks nemesis. But for many Christian traditions, such efforts, executed by a will to power isolated from God and our fellows, are condemnable. They are sinful, as they elevate human agency to an absolute, as we come to consider ourselves as masters and makers "trying to slip by God [and our fellows] on a thousand secret paths."[24] Such efforts might reveal the idolatrous will to save *ourselves* by way of the triplet of modern preoccupations, reason, will, and technique. Yet, alone (self-sufficient, solitary, and strong), we remain confronting the crises of human life and, paradoxically, "in the company of [an] apparently endless multitude of other human beings in ways we neither understand or are able to presage."[25]

Second, as stated in the first chapter and again above,

24. Karl Barth, *The Christian Life: Church Dogmatics IV.4; Lecture Fragments*, trans. Geoffrey W. Bromiley (Edinburgh: T&T Clark, 1981), 18. For further reflection on the "absolute subject" of modern preoccupation, see Karl Barth, "Man in the Eighteenth Century," in *Protestant Theology in the Nineteenth Century*, pp. 19–65. See also Scott Kirkland, *Into the Far Country: Karl Barth and the Modern Subject* (Minneapolis: Fortress Press, 2016).
25. Zygmunt Bauman, *Postmodern Ethics* (Oxford: Blackwell, 1993), 16–17.

technology is the focal fact of the present age and concerns, as Mesthene gestured to, *the organization of knowledge for the purpose of accomplishing practical aims and achievements.* Accordingly, as it might be clear by now, knowing and doing parallel the neologism *technology*, which combines the Greek *technē* (making) and *logos* (rational account). Yet making and knowing correspond further with an instrumental account that positions such *technē-logos* toward doing. Doing becomes the determinative master of technology, for without such motive, the art of knowing and the artifacts of knowledge are meaningless.

As such, doing is no longer connected to the *aretē* (moral virtue or excellence) of the subject, or craftsperson (*technitai*), who acts from a particular disposition of character and who administers knowing and making deliberately.[26] The value of the doing is disconnected, then, from the virtue of the agent, while the *autonomy* (self-sufficiency) of technology becomes a preeminent criterion. The value of doing is, in fact, located in the technological artifacts themselves, demonstrating their worth, that is, meaningfulness, by commodities they procure and produce. Therefore, knowing, making, and doing foreground the meaning of technology, which is divorced from the human agent in our current context. Techno-ontology thus reorients our considerations of value toward the preeminent power to civilize the world

26. See Aristotle, *The Nichomachean Ethics*, trans. Roger Crist (Cambridge: Cambridge University Press, 2000), 2.23–36. See also Richard Parry's essay that takes up the intellectual virtues of Aristotle: "Episteme and Techne," Stanford Encyclopedia of Philosophy, Fall 2014 ed., ed. Edward N. Zalta, https://tinyurl.com/sue7yth.

(i.e., to do) according to the image of the machine. In doing, technology proves its worth. Yet such proof is given without the cultivated virtues of an artisan, who is able not only to wield a tool with excellence but also to explain *it* (and its effects in use or disuse, whether positive and negative).

One need only to consider the pocket computers, such as Apple's iPhone, we have become so dependent on and yet, for most of us, have no idea how they are made or how they work. The modern automobile, and its digital operating systems, offers another case in point. We rely on these "intelligent" vehicles that require complex computing systems to make them function. Few of us have any ideas about how they work, which becomes most evident when they cease to function and we are at a loss to diagnose the problem or to fix them without further complex computers, digital diagnostics, and coding competencies. Our persistent ignorance and paranoia about data collection, storage, and analysis of digital media serves as a final example. Such data is sold, bought, and put to work so as to tailor each of our individual experiences of the internet and internet advertising, possibly coercing a sense of needs and desires that perpetuate further consumption.

Third, we must consider the pedagogy of techno-ontology. Rather, I think it important to interrogate the ways that modern technology educates or trains us, even unwittingly. Technology claims our habits and constrains our experiences, giving rise to mediated or participatory performances that affect the way we not only engage with but also think about everything. That is to say, modern technology invites its uptake and usage, which excites further uptake and usage, demanding performative attention to the ways such artifacts are to be deployed and their commodities enjoyed. The pedagogy of techno-ontology concerns the ways we participate in and are trained to prioritize technology.

The examination of such mediating education might be explained, in part, by Herbert Marcuse (1898–1979). In his *One Dimensional Man*, Marcuse echoes the Heideggerian claim of this volume: the essence of technology is not technological in any conventional sense. But the ubiquity of technology, its commodities, and its immanent and participatory pedagogy have prescribed patterns of thought resulting in one-dimensional thinking.[27] As Marcuse himself explains,

> [The technological society] becomes a way of life. It is a good way of life—much better than before—and as a good way of life, it militates against qualitative change. Thus emerges a pattern of one-dimensional thought and behavior in which ideas, aspirations, and objectives that, by their content, transcend the established universe of discourse and action are either repelled or reduced to terms of this universe. They are redefined by the rationality of the given system and of its quantitative extension.[28]

He continues, "The trend may be related to a development in scientific method: . . . The common feature is a total empiricism in the treatment of concepts; their meaning is restricted to the representation of particular operations and

27. Douglas Kelner, "Introduction," in *One Dimensional Man*, by Herbert Marcuse (London: Routledge, 2007), xvi.
28. Marcuse, *One Dimensional Man*, 14.

behavior." As such, Marcuse would argue that individuals are propagandized in ways that consume the individual, conforming the ways each one comes not only to reason but also to see the world. For Marcuse, technology and mass production (the mechanisms of capital) have enabled the technological rationality to indoctrinate persons as such.

We are convinced of the truth and beauty of technology because of the dependability and disburdening outcomes of technological artifacts. We use these artifacts, and their commodities are produced efficiently. We learn of technology's value, inversely conditioned by economies of time and effort, and are convinced of its potential repeatability in each and every area of our lives.

The participatory elements and the obvious benefits of the technological society, as stated previously, make it difficult to allay the effective pedagogy of technological rationality. Thus, such rationality consumes us, or as Heidegger says, *enframes* us. Everything in society, Marcuse would lament, is being operationalized, rationalized, and brought to order. Technological rationality, and its enframing, creates and sustains a "rational" monoculture, where everything is accounted for, delimited as objective, and where the irrationality of creative thinking is discouraged.

Marcuse laments that, when one's creative thinking is muted and conformed to order, our needs are defined for us, and our efforts to acquire those needs created, whether such needs are true. Consider, again, the smartphone, which I did not possess until I was well into my thirties. Regardless, after a reticent purchase, it quickly became something I seemed to need in order to communicate with others, to stay connected to my family and friends, and to never get lost while driving (even though I never did get lost while driving before my smartphone!). Unceremoniously, we seem to all have smartphones irrespective of our profession, age, or socioeconomic status. Unwittingly, we have become so attached to them that they are ready at hand, extensions of our identities.[29] As Marcuse argues, everything becomes confined within and conformed to these determinative boundaries of the technological monoculture. One-dimensional thought is cultivated accordingly.

So how should one respond?

Should humankind forcibly hold back progress or reconcile itself to suppressing creative urges? Should humanity stop technological progress altogether? Or, recognizing resistance is futile, should humanity surrender to the determinative powers?

The Possible Impossibility of Resistance

Before we are able to respond to such questions, we must continue to think about the determinative powers of technology. Such thinking might illuminate the ways that humans have been conformed by techno-ontology and obstructed from asking whether such questions are valid or whether other, perhaps fundamental, questions ought to be asked instead.

29. Michael Lynch, "Leave My iPhone Alone: Why Our Smartphones Are Extensions of Ourselves," *The Guardian*, February 19, 2016, https://tinyurl.com/ryd39lk.

Let us consider, therefore, an example from the institution of medicine: various interventions using contemporary technologies, biomedical modalities, and the like are encouraged, if not considered morally required, to effect, restore, and/or advance human capacity. Some have argued that the goal of modern medicine is to pursue knowledge, technology, and skill so as to attenuate disease, to alleviate suffering, and to sustain life—to provide the way toward complete physical, social, and mental health and to secure peace, security, and happiness.

When the limits of biology are presented and interventions determined futile or absent, modern medicine has promoted the means to control the experiences and expressions of death, as in Canada and other jurisdictions, through medical-assistance-in-dying legislation and clinical application. Consider the way in which a physician has come to consider the body abutted by death and the principal role of the medical institution: writing of physician *know-how* in our current milieu, Jeffrey Bishop argues that physicians encumbered by the pragmatics of medicine conditioned through the imperative of technology have followed the trajectory set by the modern sciences.[30] They have followed the ontology prevailing in contemporary medicine, which reduces the human body and the practice of medicine to mere mechanics, now disciplined by market metaphors.[31] Thusly,

30. Jeffrey Bishop, *The Anticipatory Corpse: Medicine, Power, and the Care of the Dying* (Notre Dame: University of Notre Dame Press, 2011).
31. Jacob Blythe and Farr Curlin, "'Just Do Your Job': Technology, Bureaucracy, and the Eclipse of Conscience in Contemporary Medicine," *Theoretical Medicine and Bioethics* 39, no. 6 (2018): 431–52.

we come to see things not in themselves but in their service to the means of technique—both power and utility. For Bishop, the power wrought from the knowledge of the human body to advance medical arts and sciences has been cultivated from the study of the corpse. It is the ideal form, the base raw material through which one learns to animate its parts by way of biomedical technique and technological intervention. Living human persons are equivalent to corpses, awaiting animating intervention when sickly and infirmed. The body is a mere machine awaiting mechanical intervention.[32] All the while, the technologically conditioned marketplace of medicine merely bureaucratizes the exchange of goods and services.

So, with an interest in knowing *how* the body functions, physicians, among other health professionals and scientists, have been distanced from the subject of study. This is done, as it is argued, to *understand* the object of enquiry: to use it, to manipulate it, and, ultimately, to improve on it. Many have located such a disposition as originating within the modern project and the corresponding technocratism, which has determined the human body as an object to master, necessitating an ontological narrative that renders an

32. For further reflection on the machine metaphors that coerce a way to see the human body as constituent parts and problems, where the heart is a pump and the brain a thinking machine, and creatures, as with machines, are thought to be "healed by a sort of mechanical tinkering," see Wendell Berry's essay "Health is Membership." Delivered as a speech at a conference, "Spirituality and Healing," Louisville, Kentucky, October 17, 1994. The speech is available at http://www.tipiglen.co.uk/berryhealth.html.

identical perspective. In this way the body's potentiality is turned toward what some have argued are its Baconian ends.

For many of us, such mastery has proven reliable. We are, after all, proficient in our palliative treatment of various chronic diseases, such as the implementation of chronic hemodialysis; successful in our advance to curb the transmission of many infectious diseases, including remediating the advance of the human immunodeficiency virus; and showing promise at the fringes of biomedical enquiry and application related to genomic medicine and predictive diagnostic competencies acquired with machine learning. With each of these serving as examples, one might already see the justification.

By these few examples within the four walls of biomedical science and practice, it makes sense that contemporary society has come to value such a particular kind of knowing as *the* principal epistemology. We have come to judge it positively by its fruits; so the argument goes: modern sciences and corollary technological production have had visible and tangible results that other humanistic disciplines, such as theology and philosophy, literature and the arts, cannot hope to achieve. Because knowledge of the natural world around us has brought with it power to control our environment, it has been able to transform the experience and expression of human life (and death), such that we have become greatly disburdened.[33] It is no wonder that people

33. J. V. Langmead Casserley, *The Fate of Modern Culture*, Signposts 1 (Westminster, UK: Dacre, 1940), 9–10.

of all backgrounds "come away with the vague impression that science [and technology as it is commonly understood] is exalted far above all other kinds of knowledge."[34] It is no wonder that corresponding technology is praised, and resistance to it thwarted as shortsighted, neo-Luddite, irrational, or, worse, morally repugnant.

It is no wonder that humanity has participated in the pedagogy of technique, while fashioning idols of the machine, in whose image we depend and are conformed.

Human being is no longer a being who is simultaneously finite and infinite, a being who was created a little lower than the angels (Heb 2:7–9), or a being whose human condition is both bodily and soulish at once, not even a being struggling over the existential paradox that we are both gods and worms;[35] but *the* being hypostasized to concrete form and function, determined as a mere object to be observed and put to use.

In this way technology is the ontology of our age.

34. Casserley, *Fate of Modern Culture*, 11.
35. Abraham Maslow, *The Psychology of Being* (New York: Harper & Row, 1968), 94. On being simultaneously finite and infinite, see Søren Kierkegaard, *Sickness unto Death* (Princeton: Princeton University Press, 1941), 9. On being both bodily and soulish, see Basil, *On the Human Condition*, trans. Nonna Verna Harrison (Yonkers, NY: St. Vladimir's Seminary Press, 2005).

3

———

Disordered Being, Dislocated Freedom

I began the first chapter by thinking about techniques of writing and the crafting of opening sentences that pique interest and provoke further reading. I turn again to writing and to the devices that we use to communicate our words—the devices that shape our speech but also occlude our communication.

Such devices as my computer and the software with which I have prepared this manuscript are used to type, to delete, to autocorrect, and to save the words I have conjured. By the time this manuscript becomes a book, my words will have been further disciplined by the devices of the publisher, which conform the font style, type settings, and formatting to an institutional standard and aesthetic convention before it is printed, packaged, marketed, and distributed. Such devices are used to increase the efficiency of writing, while also depersonalizing print for the sake of legibility and uniformity—and perhaps utility and profitability. I wonder whether the impact of my words, the forcefulness with which I communicate an idea, and the affective nuances that reveal or conceal meaning and intent are lost in the process. That is to say, I wonder whether meaningful communication is dislocated from printed word in a technologically manufactured product, which, like this book, is packaged and sold to readers. I wonder whether a book examining the question of technology is hampered in any way by the devices used to bring this book to one's eyes.

I am not the only one who has asked these questions in the context of discussions on technology. Martin Heidegger expressed contempt for the proliferation of mechanical typewriter usage rather than *das Handwerk* (work of the hand) many years prior. With the advent of the typewriter, Heidegger's concern is that "[the word] no longer comes and goes by means of the writing hand, the properly acting hand, but by means of the mechanical forces it releases."[1] Thought expressed through the body is interrupted by the mechanical prosthesis that limits and constrains thought to a stereotypical form.

Responding to Heidegger's concerns, Jacques Derrida

---

1. Martin Heidegger, *Parmenides*, trans. André Schuwer and Richard Rojcewicz (Bloomington: Indiana University Press, 1998), 81.

(1930–2004) presses the point that all such work of the hand is, and has at all times been done, with the use of instruments—handwriting, for example, does often require pen and paper, after all: "When we write 'by hand,'" he says in an interview for *La Quinzaine Littéraire* in August 1996, "we are not in the time before technology; there is already instrumentality, regular reproduction, mechanical iterability. So it is not legitimate to contrast writing by hand and 'mechanical' writing, like a pretechnological craft as opposed to technology."[2] Derrida further points out, against Heidegger's concerns, that mechanical typing, whether on a typewriter or computer, is "manual" and "doesn't bypass the hand."[3] For Derrida, such adoption of devices does not diminish the *Handwerker*, whether a thinker communicating her thoughts by a mechanical (or digital) writing tool or a carpenter fashioning a log for lumber with a mechanical mill and plane.

Derrida is right to suggest that the body is still used in the execution of the typed production of the word. He is also right to suggest that even the use of pen or pencil, quill or brush, is a form of tool usage. For that matter, the hand itself can also be thought as a tool to bear witness to the word, even in the drawing of a line in the sand. But Heidegger's point remains: to focus on the variety of devices, how they are used and what they produce, is to find one's gaze focused toward the conventional definition of technology that conceals, rather than reveals, its essential nature.

2. Jacques Derrida, "The Word Processor," in *Paper Machine*, trans. Rachel Bowlby (Stanford: Stanford University Press, 2005), 20.
3. Derrida, "Word Processor," 20–21.

So what is Heidegger's concern?

The creative word of the thinker is subdued by the homogeneity of the formed script restricted by the keys and typebars, ribbons, carriages, and other parts of typewriters. Alternatively, we might think that such script is merely selected, in an illusion of freedom, on one's computer software with the click of a mouse, the stroke of a key, and the binary whirring of zeros and ones. The creative word of the thinker, laid bare in its fullness when handwritten with variety of style and aesthetic expression, is left uniform and flattened out, readied to stand alongside all other printed pages. We now have typed words ordered further by uniform standards by ever-fewer conglomerate presses, although with the corresponding illusion of many branded imprints. The words set and produced on the printed page become indistinguishable from their authors, for the mechanization of writing from the mechanical typewriter through to its digital analogues "makes everyone look the same."[4]

Such a claim of homogeneity might seem hyperbolic when thinking about writing a research paper or preparing a manuscript for publication. But consider this statement from Heidegger: "[Type]writing . . . conceals the handwriting and thereby the character."[5] When handwritten, the

---

4. Heidegger, *Parmenides*, 81. At times, I remain ever frustrated by this reality, especially when looking on the unpleasant font type and type setting of some publications (including some of my own). Yet I am quite sure that my own handwriting, with its particular aesthetic and creative revealing (a euphemism for its utter sloppiness and indecipherability), would not be preferable.

5. Heidegger, *Parmenides*, 81.

revealed script is able to carry with it a sense of the person and personality behind the penned prose or poetry, revealing the emotional landscape in which one has written an original word. Haste and frustration, or patience and caution, for example, can be seen on the page; changes in strokes and pressures alter the weight and bearing of lines and letters, while artful flourishes, slants, and the like add further variety to the gradient, structure, and concavity of handwritten script. Handwriting can be neat, orderly, and symmetrical, or it can be messy, rushed, and irregular. It can be all of these, and more, in a single handwritten letter, let alone a lengthy manuscript. But efficient *type* and not particular *Handwerk* is the convention imposed on us by the advent and advantage of the machine.

Consider further: for many school-aged children, caught up by our technological age, homogenous text, further reduced by the efficiency of SMS language (i.e., LOL, ROTFL, etc.) and digitally produced emojis, becomes the efficient means of expressing, for example, middle-school romantic interest. Every expression is now the same save for the order of characters one might string together in a sort of shorthand communication. While some of these digital natives might never learn to handwrite in or to read cursive form, it is an unfortunate risk that these same young people might never experience the giving or receiving of carefully crafted notes that express adoration and flirtatious affection. Notes passed inefficiently by human hands. Clandestine gestures passing the note from hand to hand, across desks, through hallways, and in cafeterias. Notes dropped, picked up, and stuffed into pockets and packs. Notes delayed on desks, averting detection by the eagle eyes of a teacher or a tattle-tale. Notes eventually delivered and read. Notes given, anticipating response—but a response delayed by the ringing of the academic bell, a range of unfamiliar emotions, and the felt need to return the well-crafted note with another. Till tomorrow, then: an anxious, sleepless night.[6]

Nevertheless, I must admit, I am quite pleased not to have prepared this manuscript by my own handwork with paper and pen. Neither do I miss the embarrassment of a mismanaged love note in transit, read aloud in class (or worse still, retrieved by someone else, a person you exchanged messages with the week prior).

Yet I understand it necessary to consider the imposition. Such imposition concerned Heidegger. Technology imposes itself on us: "Even if we do not actually operate [a particular] machine, it demands that we regard it if only to renounce and avoid it. This situation is constantly repeated everywhere, in all relations of modern man to technology. Technology is entrenched in our history."[7] Few resist its advance and advantage. Yet one must raise the question: Is such entrenched history actually a crisis? Does technology disor-

---

6. Of course, as my research students have informed me, such anxiety has been merely replaced by the need and desire for immediate gratification and response. It seems people find themselves scrutinizing their phones and social-media accounts incessantly, checking for a reply. Impatience is habituated, as delays or omissions in response are experienced. Such delays contribute to other psychological distresses as well.

7. Heidegger, *Parmenides*, 86.

der our being? Does the demand that technology makes on us dislocate our freedom?

To be sure, the meaning of technology that I have described here requires a wide lens to capture. Technology, or techno-ontology, as I have preferred, concerns the ways that we have been caught up and conformed to the implicit pedagogy of technique, which trains our gaze on objects that domesticate, discipline, or destroy these same objects. The crisis sketched to this point is one in which all *things*, including humans as *things*, have been enframed by the technological rationality and its material performance of knowing-making-doing, which intends to dominate the cosmos, both within (ourselves) and without (everything and everyone else).

Berdyaev puts it this way, while tracing human history through the Renaissance to the modern period: we are at present, with the advent of the machine, concerned "to conquer and master the natural forces with a view to transforming them into an instrument of human aims, interests, and happiness." Berdyaev's observation might be thought to be repeated by Mesthene's definition, which suggests technology is the organization of knowledge for the purpose of accomplishing practical aims and achievements. But Berdyaev continues, arguing that the "conquest and subjection of external nature brings about a change in human nature itself; and, by its creation of a new environment, modifies not only nature but man himself. Human nature undergoes radical change."[8] For Berdyaev, our habits of conquest and subjection, our habits of mastery and technique, change us, and we risk becoming as the machine.[9]

But this transition, for Berdyaev, is cause for critical apprehension, because the machine—the technological reconstruction of nature, including human nature—paradoxically liberates and enslaves human being. The liberating impacts of technology make it difficult to offer critiques that compel the subject to do more than reflect. The terrible powers of technology to enslave our reasoning, our will, and our creativity become even more challenging to reveal.

If human being is changed to the point of it being enslaved, it must be shown where and how this happens. Accordingly, the following will examine the technique of dehumanization, which will show the *antihumanism* of the modern project.[10]

8. Nicholas Berdyaev, *The Meaning of History*, trans. George Reavey (San Rafael, CA: Semantron, 2009), 151.
9. Beyond familiar technological conformation, one might consider the inhuman processes of education. The idea that we are trained to present ourselves as marketable is a case in point. As Marie-Élise Zovko and John Dillon have observed, individual flourishing has become dependent on how we position ourselves advantageously in relationship to the economic machinery of the present time. See Zovko and Dillon, "Humanism vs. Competency: Traditional and Contemporary Models of Education," *Educational Philosophy and Theory*, 50, no. 6/7 (2018): 554–64 (555).
10. Rémi Brague highlights antihumanism in his examination of the failure of the modern project. The transition from humanism to antihumanism is relatively swift, as the ambitions of humanity led toward its suicide, its *extinction* (Brague, *Kingdom of Men*, 201–11).

Revealing the Technique(s) of Dehumanization

The term *dehumanization* has been used on several occasions already in this volume, although it has not yet been clearly defined. Many have labored to understand dehumanization in our modern context. The content of dehumanization has focused rightly on the reduction of human beings to things, to objects. It has focused on the disciplining of the human agent into the scaffolding of technique, whether by bureaucracy or machinery or otherwise. Such a focus is not unfamiliar. For example, Martha Nussbaum has spoken of dehumanization in terms of the (sexual) objectification of others; instrumentality, ownership, inertness, and fungibility, for example, are some characteristic markers.[11] Each of these markers shares with the mechanical logic of technological rationalities and instrumentalizing of human labor introduced previously. Critic of psychiatric medicine and psychiatric physician Thomas Szasz (1920–2012) is well known for his argument that modern psychiatric classification in itself is a dehumanizing discipline because it has involved a "mechanomorphic" logic that "thingifies" persons, reducing each one to a "defective machine."[12]

The classification of persons in terms that reduce the complexity of being to a delimited range of capacities or objective features is common to these thinkers, among

---

11. Martha Nussbaum, *Sex and Social Justice* (Oxford: Oxford University Press, 1999).
12. Thomas Szasz, *Idolatry and Insanity: Essays on the Psychiatric Dehumanization of Man* (London: Calder & Boyans, 1976), 200.

others. The result of their work, in many cases, serves to explain either dehumanization or, to a lesser degree, infrahumanization (i.e., a sort of stereotyping that prioritizes one group as being more human than another, which is less human). Similarly, the present task is to illuminate the problem of dehumanization incumbent to a world shaped by techno-ontology.

For Berdyaev, the modern person has been determined by an instrumental logic of technique. The human person has been shaped into an image of technique, caught up in a kind of mechanical performance, which determines a commitment to technological rationalities (ways of thinking) and imperatives (obligations of doing). Performing these rationalities and imperatives affects such persons, conforming them accordingly. Berdyaev suggests, therefore, that human beings are necessarily dehumanized in the advance of the technological determination and its objectifying gaze. He concludes, "That modern technics are dehumanizing man and turning him into a mere technical function is clear to everyone, and . . . is everywhere recognized."[13]

I find Berdyaev most helpful for the way he notes that it is an exercise of hubris to use modern sciences and techniques to understand nature for the purposes of utility and power. The constructed and organized world of the modern milieu habituates the knower to become also the known—an objec-

13. Berdyaev, *Fate of Man*, 37. Rémi Brague might suggest that modernity, in this way, reveals the ways that humanity is humiliated, enslaved, and mystified all the while in pursuit of acclaim, freedom, and enlightenment (*Kingdom of Men*, 141–211).

tive *it* to be put to work for the purposes of technical ends, that is, power and utility, as described previously.

Technology is not neutral. It can slip from human agency and become determinative over human being; it renders humanity a mere cog enslaved to the pedagogy and procedure of machinery. Human freedom, therefore, is at stake.

French philosopher Michel Henry laments in *La Barbarie* (*Barbarism*), "Without knowing of life and its own interests, science is placed in a nearly inconceivable solitude. This solitude of science is technology. . . . When science takes itself to be alone in the world and acts in that way, it becomes *la technique* [in that it reduces all things to objective form, to be known and mastered, thus, controlled]."[14] So, in the solitude of science, all of life becomes reducible to the mathematical and the mechanical. Freedom and creativity of life are replaced by the homogeneity and efficiency of form—love is replaced by order.[15] Culture, rather the particularity of various cultures past through present, is lost. For Henry, this is the image of barbarism—the image of our technological age, sequestered from the bountiful peculiarities of life itself.

But further questioning perhaps remains: What are the techniques of such enslavement? How are we dehumanized?

Jacques Ellul's analysis of technology, and the technological society, regards human being as that which is at risk in the modern pursuit for power, reified in the advent and advantage of technologies. The characteristics of the

14. Henry, *Barbarism*, 38, 42.
15. To put it differently, further delimiting the meaning of barbarism, dialogue, i.e., conversation, is arrogated by monologue (Brague, *Curing Mad Truths*, 101–15).

technological society become the locus for understanding the techniques of dehumanization. Rationality, artificiality, automation, monism, and universality are among some of the principal features, chief among them rationality and autonomy.

Concerning rationality, Ellul argues that wherever applied, *la technique* tends to introduce a particular discretion, which disciplines that which is spontaneous or determined as irrational. The technological rationality, or the operative mechanical theory, excludes spontaneity and creative agency, while its logic relies on calculable precision that reduces all phenomena, means, and instruments to the schema or logic of the machine.

By such logic, nature is relieved of its peculiar qualities and conditioned to form: the "treeness" of a particular tree, as Heidegger might imagine, is reduced to an atomized description of model and measure, a being caught up by the essential dimensions of a given species or genus. Of course, an equivalent description is made of other objects of modern enquiry, whether a hazelnut, a hedgehog, or a human being. Thus, one in the technological society, alongside other objects of interest, is one relieved of one's human qualities. The particularity of becoming, whether a tree, an animal, or a person, is reduced to an array of being measured and classified, and put to work for practical aims and purposes. One might see this played out through the novel engagements of genetic medicine and machine learning, where biological life is reduced to a cartography of genes, the bare facts of existence, that correlate to particular physical and psychical phenomena that can be further itemized and categorized, coded and collated for both prediction (of particular health risks and desires) and production (the remaking of biological phenomena according to medical evidence, technological and pharmacological aims, and personal wishes).

Romano Guardini (1885–1968) puts it this way: "The technological mind sees nature as an insensate order, as a cold body of facts, as a mere 'given,' as an object of utility, as raw material to be hammered into useful shape."[16] Therefore, with the operative and objectifying rationality conditioning one's thinking, every *thing* is denuded of its particularity and wildness. Nature, including human nature, is domesticated under the weight of such rational apparatus, a technique that justifies the construction of the world in the image of its logic.

Ellul regards the artificial construction as a challenge to nature: "The world that is being created by the accumulation of technical means is an artificial world and hence radically different from the natural world."[17] Comparatively, for Karl Barth, such preoccupation with artificiality is true for the modern human, whose modus operandi is to quite dispassionately study the natural world, the past, and the like, with an eye to form and for control. The correspondence between artificiality and the logic of technological rationality above is noteworthy. Accordingly, of the natural world, Barth writes that we have been led "to study nature scientifically and exploit it for gain. . . . It is . . . [now] most preferably a visibly idealized nature, which is meant: the stream as

16. Guardini, *End of the Modern World*, 55.
17. Ellul, *Technological Society*, 79.

a fountain, the lake as a clean and tidy pond, the woods as a park reduced to visible order, the field and the bushes and flowers as a garden, [and the like]."[18] So, as Ellul considers the effect of artificiality, he laments: "It destroys, eliminates, or subordinates the natural world and does not allow this world to restore itself or even enter into a symbiotic relation with it."[19]

For Ellul, the mechanical rationality and the idealist preoccupations with ordered form is inappropriate. Nature, including human nature, so measured and determined, is a reduced sort of nature. It is tamed, subdued, domesticated. The point of such domestication is to center and optimize nature for efficiency and usability. The pursuit of automatism, as Ellul notes, is a corollary aim of the technological society:

> When everything has been measured and calculated mathematically so that the method which has been decided upon is satisfactory from the rational point of view, and when, from the practical point of view, the method is manifestly the most efficient of all those hitherto employed or those in competi-

---

18. Barth, "Man in the Eighteenth Century," 41. Václav Havel's critique of normalization, or our technological civilization, echoes this sentiment and the artificial construction of space and social life, which we are conditioned to acquiesce: "We look on helplessly as that coldly functioning machine we have created inevitably engulfs us, tearing us away from the natural affiliations (for instance from our habitat in the widest sense of that word, including our habitat in the biosphere) just as it removes us from the experience of 'being' and casts us into the world of 'existences.'" See Havel, *The Power of the Powerless*, trans. Paul Wilson (London: Vintage, 2018), 134.

19. Ellul, *Technological Society*, 79.

tion with it, then the technical movement becomes self directing.[20]

Concomitantly, Lewis Mumford explains automatism in his
Technics and Civilization by suggesting that machines are to
be(come) automatic and unconstrained by interrupting
human limitations, whether physical or rational.[21] While
such automatism disburdens human persons of certain
effort and labor (often heralded as a positive achievement
that encourages further technological automatism as such),
the self-direction or self-sufficiency of technology imposes
itself on human persons, who are effectively stripped of
their faculty and freedom. Like Heidegger, Ellul regards such
stripping by the imposition of technique as a debasement or
a denial of being.

The denial continues as Ellul examines the assimilating
monism of *la technique*, which is, in his view, the only principle for orienting and resolving the challenges one might
encounter. For example, the organization of police in modern societies, namely, their technical powers to marshal
security, to reeducate antisocial behavior, and to keep order
in a society, exemplify the holism (monism) of technological
rationalities that promise and produce order. Ellul writes
accordingly,

> The more we mobilize the forces of nature, the more must
> we mobilize men and the more do we require order, which
> today represents the highest value. To deny this is to deny the

20. Ellul, *Technological Society*, 79–80.
21. Lewis Mumford, *Technics and Civilization* (London: Routledge & Sons,
1934), 10.

whole course of modern times. This order has nothing spontaneous in it. It is rather a patient accretion of a thousand
technical details. And each of us derives a feeling of security
from every one of the improvements which make this order
more efficient and the future safer. Order receives our complete approval.[22]

As such, the impulse of technique has produced an unstop-
pable momentum across all facets of contemporary existence. The principle of monism suggests that technology
becomes the question and the answer to resolving the problems incumbent to constructing one's world. As the questions and answers are rendered accordingly, *la technique*
increases in mass, and therefore momentum. It is an orientation described by George Grant as the dynamo—a reciprocal logic, by which an ongoing turning toward technology,
and its promise of efficiency, convinces us that "More technology is needed to meet the emergencies which technology
has produced"[23]—whether such emergencies are industrial,
social, or otherwise. Regarding the dynamo, Grant observes,
"What must be emphasized here is that the new technologies . . . have been the dominant responses to the crises
caused by technology itself."[24]

Therefore, the totalizing impact and the rate of technological change and risk, the monism of technology, has rendered it necessary to see efficient ordering of nature as the
preeminent response: "Every rejection of a technique

22. Ellul, *Technological Society*, 102–3.
23. Grant, *Technology and Justice*, 593.
24. Grant, *Technology and Justice*, 549.

judged to be bad entails the application of a new technique, the value of which is estimated from the point of view of efficiency alone."[25] Grant puts the inevitability of such technological monism this way:

> Western peoples (and perhaps soon all peoples) take themselves as subjects confronting otherness as objects—objects lying as raw material at the disposal of knowing and making subjects. . . . The result of this is that when we are deliberating in any practical situation our judgment acts rather like a mirror, which throws back the very metaphysic of the technology, which we are supposed to be deliberating about in detail. The outcome is almost inevitably a decision for further technological development.[26]

For Ellul, such monism is an interruption of the natural: "[We] now live in conditions that are less than human."[27] These conditions are the aim and the outcome of technique. We live in an age where "vast areas of life once subject to natural necessity or fate [are] now susceptible to [various] intervention," as Gerald McKenny puts it.[28] Such intervention is rather a technological interruption necessitated by the emergence of preceding technological advances. The interrupting repetition of technological resolutions to technological problems compels explanations and reveals a troubling disposition: *in technology we trust.*

Not only is trust bestowed, but it is globalized. Whether

25. Ellul, *Technological Society*, 110.
26. Grant, *Technology and Justice*, 605.
27. Ellul, *Technological Society*, 4.
28. Gerald McKenny, *To Relieve the Human Condition: Bioethics, Technology, and the Body* (Albany: State University of New York Press, 1997), 7.

because of its practical successes or its assimilating dominance, a technological society necessarily tends toward distributing itself to every geographical region of the world (or worlds, perhaps, with probing interest from governmental and private space organizations exploring interstellar projects involving the terraformation of Mars, for example). It does so as part of its terraforming orientation, constructing its world accordingly—making sure all other worlds fit into its machinations, convinced that such conformation is "both reasonable and just."[29]

As a constructive enterprise, techno-ontology has, therefore, "required changes in what we think is good, what we think good is, how we conceive sanity and madness, justice and injustice, rationality and irrationality, beauty and ugliness."[30] One need only to consider the growing advocacy and development for and deployment of battlefield drones—drones that produce the good of a "sanitary" (and perhaps just, rational, and beautiful) war juxtaposed to the madness of live, bodily combat. The aim of the technological society, then, is to expand its world-making tendencies and outcomes, such that every sphere of human experience is turned to order and manufactured to form.[31]

Ellul considers such globalization to reflect a principal of

29. Guardini, *End of the Modern World*, 60.
30. Grant, *Technology and Justice*, 604.
31. Michel Henry might regard such metastatic progress of technology this way: "All that can be said is that if technologies *a*, *b*, *c*, are the givens that lead to the technology *d*, this latter will be produced inevitably as their result; it does not matter by whom or where. . . . The technological world thus spreads like a cancer" (*Barbarism*, 54).

civilization, which homogenizes the particularity and diversity of cultures, aligning them to technical principles. Technology behaves like a clandestine tyrant, absorbing culture into a great totalitarian homogenous whole and putting to work those it seeks to dominate.[32] Max Horkheimer and Theodor Adorno have also observed the tyranny of such rationality and the subsequent culture industry that aims toward social uniformity as normative and objective formulation as a mode of mastery.[33] Accordingly, they argue that the tyrannical power, also observed by Ellul and others, subverts any insubordination and deviation from the formula established as socially normative or as a civilizational necessity. Not to conform means to be rendered powerless, an outsider, incompetent, or irrational—a technique of dehumanization.

Not only do these techniques of degradation raise many questions about human freedom, but more fundamentally, they call into question the reality of autonomy in the technological society. Whose autonomy? To what limit?

Illusions of Autonomy, Enslaving Creativity

In Ellul's *The Technological Society*, no individual part of a given system may maintain itself distinct from the technical ensemble. This includes human persons assimilated by the juggernaut of technique. Where a system functions properly without human guidance or creative input, humans are

32. Ellul, *Technological Society*, 284–91.
33. Horkheimer and Adorno, *Dialectic of Enlightenment*, 133.

observed and used as tools (or, ideally, excluded altogether as automaticity, introduced earlier). But where human persons remain a part of the functional system, each individual is expected to capitulate to the system, to accommodate oneself, and not to allow oneself to express any particularity or creativity. The celebration or inclusion of human autonomy in such a system is an inclusion of an illusory form of autonomy. The person is put to work and disciplined by order and form determined by techno-ontology (by the *autonomy of technology*).[34] Thus, in a society conformed by technique, it is not surprising to see even moral and political rhetoric conformed by the efficient force of technique.[35]

34. Ellul, *Technological Society*, 133–47.
35. See Neal Postman, *Technopoly: The Surrender of Culture to Technology* (New York: Vintage, 1993). Similarly, Michel Henry argues provocatively that the technology thus far described has the capacity to destroy human nature, which leaves one with a profound sense of powerlessness, ultimately leading toward the annihilation of subjectivity. For Henry, this is barbarism, the consequence of the modern will to power through the quantifiable exercise of reason and technology, that is, "the omnipresent objectivism of modernity" (*Barbarism*, xvii). While there is a tendency to reduce human being to human doing, as discussed already, where the abstract and expendable laborer is only as good as she may be good *for* the instrumental apparatus, technologies incumbent to ethics and politics equally reduce persons to instruments. One might point toward rhetorical and justificatory paradigms that function mechanically, reducing all ethical and political speech to form. Moral agents are to adopt such speech if they want to be taken seriously, as morally serious agents. Those who might refuse such organized discourse risk being marginalized or removed. For further discussion on this matter, see also my *Reading Karl Barth, Interrupting Moral Technique, Transforming Biomedical Ethics* (London: Palgrave, 2015). Part of the following has been adapted from my book and is used with permission.

Consider, for example, the inclusion of *autonomy* in the familiar applied-ethics apparatuses involved in biomedical ethical decision-making. While the principle of autonomy is an oft-praised principal, frequently meant to reflect the capacity for an individual to self-determine free from coercive influence and limited by nonmaleficence (to do no harm), Berdyaev might locate autonomy as an abstract and therefore unreal criterion that isolates the individual behind the veil of an illusory freedom exercised as choice. Yet moral efficiency, the commodity of decision-making competence produced by the incumbent moral techniques, requires individual operators of the conformed moral systems to render judgments and act accordingly—this is their designated function.

Therefore, while such moral techniques continue to include the human element, a "coefficient of elasticity" remains.[36] That is, a designated role for human action, for individual decision, as imprecise as it may be, remains. For applied-ethics disciplines, the independence of the human *individual* is emphasized in order to ease the struggle of obstinate moral dilemmas, thereby locating decision-making in a sequestered rational will, a will freed from all others.

Yet the will is instrumentalized, while the moral techniques "maintain the illusion of liberty, choice, and individuality."[37] Let me explain: as Ellul observes, when considering technique, the technical criteria matter, not the human ele-

---

36. Ellul, *Technological Society*, 136.
37. Ellul, *Technological Society*, 138.

ment. He argues further that the end of technology is in fact the end for human autonomy: "Technique requires predictability and, no less, exactness of prediction. It is necessary, then, that technique prevail over the human being ... in order to wipe out the blots his personal determination introduces into the perfect design of the organization."[38]

Similarly, Horkheimer and Adorno lament such contrived morality as they discuss the nature of *schematism*. Under the determining influence of schema both revealed and concealed by modern technological society, "Everything—even the human individual, not to speak of the animal—is converted into the repeatable, replaceable process, into a mere example for the conceptual models of the system."[39] Likewise, the autonomous person subsumed under the weight of moral technique is but a rudimentary cog in the mechanics of moral decision-making—any one individual will do, so long as she takes up the conceptual models and capitulates to the grammar of the moral technique (schema that discipline and curtail even the dilemmas that the ethics are introduced to resolve). Such persons thus are no longer free; rather, such persons, whomever they might be—it no longer matters—are bound by the moral technique.

The illusion of autonomy persists.

The will, therefore, is not free to respond creatively to the problems encountered in political or moral life. Rather, the will must submit to the a priori forms illumined by the professional, political, or moral technique and rendered nec-

38. Ellul, *Technological Society*, 135, 139.
39. Horkheimer and Adorno, *Dialectic of Enlightenment*, 84.

essary by the population of leaders and decision-makers sensitive to it, rendered instead *basic* for those committed to the objectives of the common organization, whether political or moral. Dissenters are removed as irrational and uncommitted, or retributively disciplined into order. Put differently, such assembly of techniques in professional, political, and moral milieu is not intended to grapple with real persons confronted by concrete dilemmas. Rather, such techniques diminish human creativity and freedom while they convert human difference to form and construct new artificialities to be shared and implemented, necessarily.[40] The exercise of an individual rational will under the constraints of such technique is simply a conformation to the ideal form and the objectives of the technological society, which seeks to oppose the world in which it exists.

This opposition is often occluded by the successes of the world conformed by technique. Nevertheless, the particular preoccupation with the idea that knowledge (or information) ought to bring power, and such power ought to be used

40. See Havel's *Power of the Powerless*, and the greengrocer's hanging of a window sign that repeats the familiar communist slogan, "Workers of the World, Unite!" The action to display the sign is a determined response as the systems of totalitarianism conform or normalize irresponsibility. "Havel's point is that normalization is unfreedom because it coaxes you to do the things that you are unreflexively inclined to do anyway: drink the bad beer others are brewing, listen to the bad music that others are playing, repeat the phrases that other are saying. Normalization speaks to the sensibilities that feel personal but are general, suppressing your individuality before it can be expressed in any notable actions." See Timothy Snyder, "Introduction," in *Power of the Powerless*, xv. Havel's normalization is a synonym of the technique, or techno-ontology, being studied here.

to subdue nature, reveals the dehumanizing trends or anti-humanism that techno-ontology bolsters.

Power Dominates Our Imagining Better

Horkheimer and Adorno articulate well the preoccupation with knowledge-comes-power, by which humans seek to acquire objective information about material nature in order to put it to work, to make something of it, and to dominate the object of inquiry.[41] This capacity to control is prized by many, among others those sensitive to the objectives of the modern preoccupation with power.

Such control is achieved as one comes to possess further knowing. Knowledge secures a particular order. Yet in the procurement of such order, human beings distance themselves from the objects of study, including themselves. It is done to *understand it* so as to *manipulate it* to suit the objectives of technology. Even the human body has become an object to control, as though the body's potential and meaning were determined by one's capacity to exercise knowing, that is, power, over it.[42]

The labor to exercise and advance such power is valued by

41. Horkheimer and Adorno, *Dialectic of Enlightenment*, 2–6.
42. This should remind us of Heidegger's references to *enframing*. It is the concept that describes how technology has become the lens through which the world is seen as an object of limitless technological manipulations. The latest advances in biomedical sciences, especially genetics and genomics, and information technologies exemplify this particular orientation toward pushing the boundaries of human finitude and exerting the power of biomedical technology over our bodies.

conventional medical professionals. But the Baconian project is not merely settled to advance power over infectious disease, chronic illness, and experiences of pain and suffering. Instead, some have set their objectifying gaze on the greatest of human problems, that is, involuntary death.[43] The possibility of restoring human capacity and reversing the deleterious effects of aging, disease, and dysfunction is no longer mere science fiction.

With the exercise of human will disciplined by technological rationality and intervention, humanity has time and again demonstrated a particular capacity to attend to the body, and its limitations, as a problem to resolve. Many biomedical successes can be noted, but current attention turns to aging and death, considered preeminent problems to resolve. As Tom Creo in the film *The Fountain* (directed by Darren Aronofsky, 2006) puts it: "Death is a disease. It's like any other. And there's a cure, a cure—and I will find it."

To understand aging and death as such, as a problem to resolve, one must relinquish an understanding of death as an inevitable natural phenomenon of biological life or the existential limit to our earthly human becoming. Instead, death must be remodeled, if you will, as the ultimate disease to conquer through biotechnological means.[44] The purpose of such pursuit is to arrest the biological limitations of the

---

43. For example, the mission of the LongeCity organization (also known as the Immortality Institute) is to "conquer the blight of involuntary death" (see www.Longecity.org and www.ImmInst.org).
44. Joanne Martin and Michael Sheaff, "The Pathology of Ageing: Concepts and Mechanisms," *The Journal of Pathology* 211, no. 2 (2007): 111–13 (111).

human brain and body while enhancing others, transcending our present human existence. That is to say, the goal is to master technology, including the technology of the body, to such a degree that humanity might succeed the boundaries of biological existence. In this way, one might fulfill the familiar dictum introduced earlier: *knowledge is power*.

While such aims might be considered normative, a nihilistic undercurrent might persist—even if it remains occluded by the triumphs of technological medicine. It might be that undergirding such pursuits for health and longevity remains a great discontentment cultivated from the modern aim to conquer death and achieve, as some portend, physical immortality. Such discontentment might be thought as contempt—an antihuman posture, to be blunt.

Let me explain, briefly, while focusing on the posthuman pursuits of contemporary scientific and biotechnological endeavor: the will-to-power is pursued through research and development into the chimeric interface between biological, digital, and mechanical phenomena, or through the potentiality to become liberated from biology altogether: "People of the world, unite. You have nothing to lose but your biological chains!"[45] The discourse surrounding possible human futures is without a single representative text or school of thought, but the variety of voices is united by the stories that cultivate modern being given unto technology.

The general posture concerning human futures is one in pursuit of posthuman liberation, expressed by acquisition

45. Simon Young, *Designer Evolution: A Transhumanist Manifesto* (Amherst, MA: Prometheus Books, 2006), 31.

of new powers and progress. It is a "belief in overcoming human limitations through reason, science, and technology."[46] Posthumans are "possible future beings whose basic capacities so radically exceed those of present humans as to be no longer unambiguously human by our current standards."[47] *Posthuman* serves as an umbrella term for the ranging voices who pursue and present possible posthuman futures or variable intermediary forms of possible beings, who take advantage of synthetic artificial intelligences, enhanced uploads, and small but cumulatively profound augmentations to a biological human using, in part, nanotechnologies, genetic engineering, neural interfaces, and the like.[48] Increasing reliance on machine learning and artificial intelligences ensures haste in collecting large swaths of data and efficient processing, intended to proffer the predictive accounts of future expressions of data (i.e., to help project the probable unfolding of our genetic morphologies and physiologies, bodily structures and functions, which can be interrupted by rearranging or editing such data, altering the probable outcomes).

Put differently, transhumanism might be regarded as "the intellectual and cultural movement . . . of improving the human condition through applied reason" using technologies to enhance "intellectual, physical, and psychological

---

46. Young, *Designer Evolution*, 15.
47. Nick Bostrom, "The Transhumanist FAQ: A General Introduction," World Transhumanist Association, https://tinyurl.com/y8nmzos2.
48. Jeanine Thweatt-Bates, "The Transhumanist Manifesto," in *Cyborg Selves: A Theological Anthropology of the Posthuman*, ed. Roger Trigg and J. Wentzel van Huysteen (London: Routledge, 2012), 41–65 (41–42).

capacities." The transhumanist is one who "sees the current state of the human in an evolutionary transition, on a transitory journey from ape to human to posthuman. . . . The goal of transhumanism, then, is the posthuman. The posthuman is a future being—a person—who constructs herself out of various technologies."[49]

Such thinking reveals a relative disdain for human being and the conditions of human existence as we experience them, including those limits often bounded by fate and finitude. In other words, life (and death) is not learned through trials, failures, and personal achievements; instead, it must be managed and mastered, removing any element that is out of human control or a threat to bodily integrity. The art of living is no longer a commitment to human flourishing but an endless pursuit of technological mastery.

The human being as it may be experienced by you and I, for the transhumanist, is thus a transitory thing to be shaped and remade according to the ideals set out by a technological imaginary. The human being is but a means to bring about the advent of higher beings, those conjured by the image of technological permanence and progress. Its image is a technological reimagining of Nietzsche's *Übermensch*, the antihumanist ideal: "How poor indeed is a human being! . . . How ugly, how gasping, how full of concealed shame! . . . Human being, however, is something that must be overcome."[50] Human being must be transcended.

49. Jeffrey Bishop, "Transhumanism, Metaphysics, and the Posthuman God," *The Journal of Medicine and Philosophy* 35, no. 6 (December 2010): 700–720 (700–701).
50. Friedrich Nietzsche, *Thus Spoke Zarathustra: A Book for All and None*, ed.

But to what end? Technology, of course.

Such rhetoric crafted around the imagery of better is therefore no cultural movement. It is a reiteration of techno-ontology turned toward the making of *useful* human objects. Techno-ontology has thus coerced our senses and sensibilities, turning our gaze away from human ends and toward industrial means, digital competencies, and targeted capital investments, such that the incumbent economic program (industrial capitalism) and the emerging political structures (digital-industrial biotechnological complex) can thrive in a perpetual technological system that can pursue both power and progress (including profit, of course) at rates of speed and evolving efficiencies that match the non-linearity of technological change.

This is, perhaps, what Berdyaev means by his repeated claims in *The End of Our Time* (1933), *The Fate of Man in the Modern World* (1935), and *The Meaning of History* (1936) that, with the climax of the First World War and the Bolshevik Revolution, the end of the Renaissance period and the completion of the modern project had arrived. Its fixation on material and mechanism coupled with haughty pride and the elevation of self-sufficiency served to generate and degrade the Renaissance or Enlightenment subject, and the modern project "*unfolds the self-destructive dialectic of humanism.*"[51] So "the triumphant advent of the machine constitutes one of

Adrian Del Caro and Robert Pippin (Cambridge: Cambridge University Press, 2006), 216.

51. Nicholas Berdyaev, "The End of the Renaissance," *Sophia: Problems of Spiritual Culture and Religious Philosophy* (1923), 21–46, https://tinyurl.com/qs4h2rm (emphasis original).

the greatest revolutions in human destiny," yet the revolution is not one aimed at human flourishing or by the creative agency of human persons. Rather, it is a revolution of the chthonic power of techno-ontology to make all things into its own image, into the material parts that are then put to work for the advent of unending technological progress.

Berdyaev's analysis, therefore, is apropos: while basking in the promise of Renaissance and Enlightenment ideations, and in our pursuit of solitude and self-mastery, we have found ourselves to be stripped of creativity and dominion, all the while being moved and formed, ruled, and enslaved.[52] Our will to power has succeeded, and power dominates.

Pessimism and the Standing Reserve

Let us turn to Heidegger, once again: as *technē* becomes increasingly understood as knowing-producing, with a principal aim of calculating efficiency, it becomes the master over and destructive of the particularity of human being (*physis*).[53] So, it is important to consider that technology is no neutral power, but a power with its own *soul*—and the hubris of humanity has created, nurtured, and liberated it. As technology becomes increasingly divorced from human subjectivity, it becomes something "other"; yet, as an *it* without measure, technology becomes a chthonic power

52. Dietrich Bonhoeffer, *Creation and Fall: A Theological Exposition of Genesis 1–3*, ed. Wayne Whitson Floyd Jr., trans. Douglas Stephen Bax, vol. 3, Dietrich Bonhoeffer Works (Minneapolis: Fortress Press, 1997), 66–67.
53. Martin Heidegger, *Introduction to Metaphysics*, trans. Gregory Fried and Richard Polt (New Haven: Yale University Press, 2000), 17–19.

ready to exert its control over all things. To think of technologies as mere instruments that do not demand particular usage but surrender to human will is misleading. Take, for example, the image of the moral neutrality of a gun, as though one has other options than violence when taking up arms. The state and status of technologies, of machines, of incessant calculative and instrumental reasoning and schematizing, does necessitate particular uses. Accordingly, learning from Heidegger, such chthonic technology must be thought of as an *instrumentum* that imposes its means on us. Yet such technology is more than mere means.[54]

The instrumentality of technology is considered to be the essential characteristic to bring forth knowledge and truth —to reveal the objectivity of production, with repeatable efficiency. Yet for Heidegger, among others whom he has influenced, modern technology brings forth the regulating, securing, and ordering of nature, including human nature, as discussed. The production of such order is also the consequence of the power of technology to determine all things into a singular, homogenous whole, where particularity disappears "into the objectlessness of standing-reserve."[55] This also goes for the disappearing particularity of persons, who become mere cogs, replaceable and instrumental, awaiting the final stage of automation, that is, the self-sufficient machine.[56] The laborer is found in the standing-reserve, wholly *enframed* or determined by technology, and

54. Grant, "Thinking about Technology," 589–606.
55. Heidegger, *Question Concerning Technology*, 19.
56. Lewis Mumford, *The Myth of the Machine: The Pentagon of Power* (New York: Harcourt Brace Jovanovich, 1964), 179.

dehumanized without vocation but required to perform general functions serving the machine. In such service to the machine, the laborer—*any* laborer, as she is expendable—is isolated from the whole event and history of work, and reduced "to a cunning hand, a load-bearing back, or a magnifying eye"[57] until no longer needed; until all of nature is stripped of its telos, and meaning becomes reserved only *for* instrumental usage. The end of technology, therefore, is the end of ends.

But is this conclusion the final word? Is the end of technology our final destiny? Is this the fate of the modern world? Is resistance and protest meaningless?

Grant was sure that technology is our destiny. Yet for Grant, pessimism, that nihilistic experience and expression of meaninglessness, is not to be heard as the final word. Resisting pessimism is possible; therefore, resisting the determining powers of technology is also possible. Consider his related words regarding pessimism and politics: in an edited interview transcript published with the journal *Grail* (March 1985), Lawrence Schmidt is interrupted by Grant's response concerning his pessimism about Canadian politics:

[Schmidt]: Your pessimism is rooted in a . . .

Grant: That's not pessimism. Let me say one word about this because I think it's imperative. Often I am called a pessimist. Anybody who believes in God (and I would say that I almost know God exists) cannot be a pessimist. The words optimism and pessimism originated with [Gottfried Wilhelm] Leibnitz and they refer to the nature of the world. I think we live in an

57. Mumford, *Myth of the Machine*, 179.

atrocious political era. *But it is God's world and if you assert that, you cannot be a pessimist.*[58]

In this, our technological age, we must learn again to "see that [technology] doesn't destroy our natures." We must learn again to become a hope-full community such that we might not become "less as a result of technological innovations."[59]

58. George Grant and Lawrence Schmidt, "An Interview with George Grant (*Grail*)," in Grant, *Collected Works of George Grant*, vol. 4, 562–82 (569).
59. George Grant, "A Giant Steps Down," in *Collected Works of George Grant*, vol. 4, 536–37 (537) (emphasis added).

PART II

Performing
the Response

4

———

Storied (In)Humanity, Performing Dissent

If you have read this book from the beginning, you will recall that I have thought about writing as a way to challenge us to think about technology. I reflected on the mechanics of writing, both the technique of the opening sentences of a book intending to hook a reader and the mechanical mediation of one's writings determined by devices such as typewriters and computers. Such thinking is connected to further reflection about the way words are strung together to tell stories. Language shaped by such stories, and stories shaped by language, reveal not only our imagination but also our world. This will be the focus for much of these final chapters.

Stories have profound ontological implications. Words, crafted as stories, often arranged as poetry or prose but not limited to such forms, describe the world and cultivate our imagination. Such words educate us: such stories discipline our senses and sensibilities, discovering both meaning and direction.[1] Stories conform our vision and transform our relation to the world, including ourselves.[2]

Yet stories are not merely recited. They are performed. It is by way of such performance, the telling, retelling, and enacting of such stories, that the world we learn to see and come to want is made. I agree with Henry Corbin (1903–78) when he writes that reality is hidden within the stories we tell. He describes this as the "precise order of reality." By the drawing out of such stories, through their imaginative re-production, reality defines and delimits the external world. "Spiritual reality [i.e., imagination] envelops, surrounds, contains so-called material reality," conforming it accordingly.[3]

However, such shaping can include misshaping. Formation can include malformation. It is malformation that concerns me when thinking about the (ubiquitous) experiences and (persistent) pedagogy of techno-ontology, with various

1. Henry Corbin, *Mundus Imaginalis, or the Imaginary and the Imaginal*, trans. Ruth Horine (Ipswich, UK: Golgonooza, 1972), 4. The original essay was published as "Mundus imaginalis ou l'imaginaire et l'Imaginal," *Cahiers internationaux de Symbolisme* 6 (1964): 3–26.
2. Stanley Hauerwas, *The Peaceable Kingdom : A Primer in Christian Ethics* (Notre Dame: University of Notre Dame Press, 1983), 29.
3. Corbin, *Mundus Imaginalis*, 1, 4.

technological artifacts "embedded in coevolving social practices, values, and institutions."[4]

I am concerned with the pervasive influence of disciplining by technology such that we are becoming as technology is making us—and seemingly unable to stop its forward march, with a momentum to provoke ongoing and widespread changes to the world around us and within.

The future of humanity, and of the world, is confronted by increasing mastery over, for example, biological phenomena now regarded as mere information technology to be hacked, manipulated, and manufactured.[5] Intelligence, thought of as a mere algorithm for data processing, has become a principal focal point of scientific and technological endeavor and of the essential aspect of being (and an aspect that some desire to enhance, to keep pace, or narrow the gap, with artificial intelligences). Bodies, whether biological or synthetic (in various forms), are thought as cumbersome, inconvenient, and inadequate.

But the possibilities of such mastery (over so-called bodies) are nothing new, save for the tools and techniques and corresponding imaginings about ideal bodies to house the whirring of techno-enhanced minds (determined as information processors) and to execute socially determined economic functions. Such bodies are regarded as objects of information to be hacked and edited to suit the technological-economic present chasing the technological-

4. Shannon Vallor, *Technology and the Virtues: A Philosophical Guide to a Future Worth Wanting* (Oxford: Oxford University Press, 2016), 5.
5. See Jamie Metzl, *Hacking Darwin: Genetic Engineering and the Future of Humanity* (Naperville, IL: Sourcebooks, 2019).

economic future. Bodies risk becoming as fodder for techno-socializing inscriptions, with compounding confusion concerning subjectivity, intellectual and physical property, and the telos of being.[6]

Such stories, that is, of bodies as constellations of malleable information and objects of control, invite great risk. The answer to such risk is not to be found in familiar ethical methodology that reduces moral reasoning to a utilitarian calculus of costs and benefits. Such reasoning is caught up by the technological rationality that techno-ontologies forge. Accordingly, such ethics cannot train us to stand in protest.

One must be wistful and wary, therefore: not all worlds imagined and built are right or good. Some such worlds are, theologically speaking, corrupt. They leave us unful-

---

6. To understand analogous inscribing, one might be wise to turn toward the works of Saidiya Hartmann, for example. See Hartmann, *Scenes of Subjection: Terror, Slavery, and Self-Making in Nineteenth Century America* (Oxford: Oxford University Press, 1997). Her penetrating examination of the construction of individuated black bodies and their subjugation, determination, and destruction by the white over-class might grant perspective here. The technologizing of bodies is as a repetition of the persistent objectivization and sociocultural and legal resolve to manufacture the political such that, whether by enslavement or by contract, coercion or consent, human persons become as mere instrumental means or resources to be used, and often used up. The wisdom from marginalized and subjugated communities, of persons determined as objects by insidious ideations and performative habituations, might offer us further perspective concerning the crisis we are confronting.

filled and bounded by promises of power and progress. Some such worlds are as the antichrist.[7]

Saying Babylon, Seeing Desires, Making the World of Bigots and Fanatics

Such power and progress also concerned distinguished Canadian scholar of literature Northrop Frye (1912–91), who delivered the second annual Massey Lectures over the radio in autumn 1962. The lectures were published in print by the Canadian Broadcasting Company with the same title, *The Educated Imagination* (1963). Frye, concluding these lectures, says the technological construction of modern-day cities, and their towers of concrete, glass, and steel, which reach skyward, are as Babel, "poised . . . to destroy any semblance of communication among human beings."[8] The destruction of communication, rather the *constructed* refusal to communicate, will render a world barbaric.[9] Recognizing the hazards, Frye, therefore, argues that opposition between technological progress and creative imagination must be given attention, and persons must take up the task of education and of culture making so that they might "find the

---

7. Brandon Gallaher, "Godmanhood vs Mangodhood: An Eastern Orthodox Response to Transhumanism," *Studies in Christian Ethics* (February 2019): 1–11.
8. David Cook, *A Vision of the New World*, ed. Arthur Kroker and Marilouise Kroker, New World Perspectives (Oxford: Oxford University Press, 1985), 18.
9. Brague, *Curing Mad Truths*, 101–15.

depowered site where the 'poet can be heard.'"[10] The response to techno-ontology as previously sketched will honor such conviction and concern.

But it is his opening lecture, "The Motive for Metaphor," that will draw our focus at this time. It narrates the uses or types of language and the reason we turn to literature to shape our vision of human civilization. Thus let me begin by introducing Frye's typologies of language:

First, the language of consciousness or awareness is one where nouns and adjectives are used to furnish a description of the objective world—the world before us, the world "set over against [us]." The world as described, Frye goes on to say, is one that "may have a shape and a meaning, but it doesn't seem to be a *human* shape or a *human* meaning." The world as it is thus assumes a sort of neutral or amoral objectivity—an objectivity that lends itself to dispassionate observation and rationality. But in relation to human desires or aims, such a world is organized by value statements. As Frye points out, the world as it is can be adjudicated passionately: "'I like this' and 'I don't like this'" about the material world are further complicated by the material world's relative position narrated as *outside* human being. The world of objective materials and motions is the site for critical existential reflection that gives rise to expressions of desire. Thus, "the feeling 'this is not a part of me' soon becomes 'this is not what I want.'"[11]

10. Cook, *Vision of the New World*, 18.
11. Northrop Frye, *The Educated Imagination*, CBC Massey Lectures (Toronto: House of Anansi, 2002), 3, 5 (emphasis added).

If the world is merely one of raw or neutral objects, objects of undesired matter and motion, objects without *human* shape or meaning (whatever that might mean), then the second level of language illuminates the words of our desires in the form of verbs: in order to _____ [in order to *accomplish practical aims and achievements*]. At this level "action speaks louder than words."[12] In this way, Frye suggests the second level of language is the language of practical sense, which illuminates the ways and means of civilization building or production. It reveals means and human activities. It is the language of the technological world in a conventional sense.

The second type of language depends on the third: the language of imagination. As Frye declares, "The world you *want* to live in is a human world, not an objective one: it's not an environment but a home; it's not the world you see but the world you build out of what you see."[13] The third mode of language, exemplified in literature, conjures the world we want to have.

Frye introduces this third mode of language while also showing the ways the three levels of languages correspond, albeit differently. He argues, for example, that the first and third levels of language move in opposite directions. Connecting science to the first and literature to the third, he suggests that while sciences begin with the external world and add imagination, literature begins in the imaginative world and becomes involved in civilization: "[Science] starts

12. Frye, *Educated Imagination*, 7.
13. Frye, *Educated Imagination*, 5 (emphasis added).

with the world as it is, [literature] with the world we want to have."[14] But both seem to converge on the second level of language, that of practical sense. This convergence is interesting given the concerns of this book and two claims Frye introduces in the lectures, so allow me to highlight the relevant concerns briefly before turning to Frye's claims.

Something is troubling about our technological age. The trouble is not with any one artifact of technology, the trouble is not with the devices we construct to allay burden, the data we procure and analyze to facilitate decision-making, or the development of projects, programs, or procedures to guarantee progress.[15] The crisis of technology that I have sketched to this point is about the essential nature of technology rather than about proliferating products and possibilities of the technological age. Technology is the ontology of our age. As such, the crisis concerns the ways that such an ontology coerces and conforms human being—the way techno-ontology, as a habituating pedagogy, trains the way we have become surveyors, manipulators, and masters

---

14. Frye, *Educated Imagination*, 9.
15. Indeed, it might be vital to examine such technologies closely, so that we might better learn to discern between those artifacts that aid human flourishing, for example, and those that both harm and dehumanize. Of course, individual artifacts of technology often help some to flourish while harming others. The analyses of such technologies therefore must be adjudicated wisely, and with both nuance and depth. One might look to Kate Ott's *Christian Ethics for a Digital Society* (London: Rowman & Littlefield, 2018) for such an analysis. Gerald McKenny's *Biotechnology, Human Nature, and Christian Ethics* (Cambridge: Cambridge University Press, 2018) offers another example.

against nature, including human nature, seeking to construct a civilization.

The crisis, therefore, concerns the moral being, fashioned by techno-ontology.

Such training leads to my interest in Frye's lectures on the educated imagination. Our imagination has been educated by—or the stories that reveal our imagination have followed after—the literature that has cultivated the modern project. Such literature has presented mathematics as the imaginative language of the sciences—and such language, as literature, "does not evolve or improve or progress."[16] It is universal and totalizing. The absolute language of such literature has seemingly united the first and third levels of language, repeating that the world "out there" *is* the world of our imagination.

Mathematics, the imaginative language of the sciences, is therefore also the language of consciousness and awareness. The language of the scientific world we observe has become identical to the imagined world we want to have. The shape and meaning of both worlds have been narrated by way of absolute integers and constructive formulas of mathematics. The world of our imaginings, which is a repetition of the world out there, can therefore *become* the world of our practical aims, too. The languages merely repeat as though their respective levels, as originally introduced by Frye, have been erased.

Those of us disciplined by modernity have been trained to see the world through the eyes of Copernicus, Kepler, and

16. Frye, *Educated Imagination*, 9.

Galileo: as Milton Scarborough says, "To know what was true of nature [of the external world] one had only to discover what was true of mathematics."[17] The measurable dimensions of shapes, positions, motions, and the like have been thought as primary qualities that illuminate what is true of the external world, permitting the illusion of the mind, of the subjective inner world of experience, to withdraw to the background (or to withdraw altogether). With the advent of information technologies and their theoretical underpinnings, we have continued to be trained to see the world through the eyes of George Boole (1815–64), Claude Shannon (1916–2001), and Lili Gatlin (1928–2017).

By the numbers we will go. A constellation of data we are.

The *poietic* dimension of stories educates our imagination, introducing us to new possibilities that have not previously existed before, that is, the novel possibility that we can, by the exercise of modern means, be free of the haunting tyranny of physical nature, as we saw in Mesthene's proposal in the first chapter. When our stories reflect the mathematical imagination of Galileo and the epistemic quest of Bacon, and the imagination is turned necessarily toward practical realization, we begin to shape or make our world, including ourselves, accordingly. We make a new world. We bring into existence that which did not exist before: a technological civilization.

The new world conformed by techno-ontology is as Babylon. After all, the one who incarnates the modern narrative

17. Milton Scarborough, *Myth and Modernity: Postcritical Reflections* (Albany: State University of New York Press, 1994), 11.

boasts of material abundance, efficient productivity, technological promise, and the like. The devotion to modern technological civilization is reinforced as one justifies its construction, pointing toward its record of securing knowledge with empirical precision (power of and through sciences) and of disburdening the masses by its capabilities to build *everything* (power of technique), offering up a world for *our* usage, "creating a [way] of privilege and exploitation."[18] Technological civilization boasts of a world where we can remain "outside history as self-made men and women . . . [in a managed world] that believes that there are no mysteries to honor, only problems to be solved," as Walter Brueggemann puts it.[19]

Many have learned to share in the grandiose horizon of this new Babylon. They set toward technology, in the conventional sense, and promise to participate in the building of it in order to secure their own futures. New Babylon, as the world wrought by human desire and production, is *their* world. It is a world of logic, observation, and mathematics, decisive features of the absolute power unveiled by the sciences and reified in machines, whether industrial, digital, political, or moral.

The argument is that the world is being *humanized* by the self-sufficient, solitary, and strong fist of human agency that has captured the potency of the sciences and advantage of technologies to put the world right—to make it significant,

18. James K. A. Smith, *Desiring the Kingdom: Worship, Worldview, and Cultural Formation* (Grand Rapids: Baker Academic, 2009), 101.
19. Walter Brueggemann, *The Prophetic Imagination*, 2nd ed. (Minneapolis: Fortress Press, 2001), 37.

according to our human desire and design.[20] The stories that have shaped us into our technological age, therefore, are stories of a will to power. Such stories train us to see not only nature but also human nature as something that must be overcome. It makes sense, then, that the foci for contemporary scientific enquiry and commercial economic investment—as exemplified in the growing interest in genetic engineering and machine learning, things that used to be on the fringes—articulate such a will to power with the promise and prestige of preference, performance, and permanence.

The possibility of bringing into existence that which has not yet existed prior is alluring. The modern narrative is intoxicating in that way. It promises freedom from "the demands of supposedly sacred orders." Such freedom, as Charles Taylor continues, "came about through the discrediting of such orders" and the inaugurating of self-governance bolstered by political rights and legal protections.[21] We are permitted, by such freedom, to create the world of our choosing—as the narrative ironically determines. Moreover, the narrative promises increasingly efficient means of relief from burden, toil, frustration, and frailty. It assures the maximization of happiness and the minimization of suffering through the administration of instrumental reason, whether by economic application or technological innovation. Cost-benefit analysis, the calculus of utility, has delivered prosperity and assurance. The out-

20. Stephen R. L. Clark, "Science Fiction and Religion," in *A Companion to Science Fiction*, ed. David Seed (Oxford: Blackwell, 2005), 95–110 (107).
21. Charles Taylor, *The Malaise of Modernity* (Concorde, ON: House of Anansi, 1992), 2–3.

comes continue to demonstrate the veracity and reliability of the modern narrative. It is a story that not only works but is (tautologically) justified.

We often overlook the hazards such a narrative cultivates. We overlook the distrust in other imaginal worlds, in other narratives, as such a narrative cultivates a technological civilization that casts aside all it cannot comprehend or master. We fail to see alternative visions of past, present, and future, as our gaze is set on mastery over the future, determining present decision-making accordingly, now through the expedient predictive trajectories of collated and scrutinized data streams.

For those of us enveloped by the ubiquity of technology, our lives "conditioned technologically," this is the civilization of our making.[22] This is the world wrought from *our* proclamations, reclamations, and configurations. We have turned our (mathematical) imaginings into (technological) actualities. We find ourselves spinning as a cog inside Grant's dynamo. Put differently, we have been introduced to modern metaphors that say *a is b*, that is, nature *is* both kinetic and kinematic detail. The metaphors of measure, in our current milieu, remind us that the world, both inside and outside our being, is a mere pattern of data awaiting analysis and reconfiguration.

The purpose of using such metaphors is to tell us what something else *is*. The motive for using metaphors in the telling of stories is to help shape our world. Or, in accordance with American modernist poet Wallace Stevens

22. Vallor, *Technology and the Virtues*, 2.

(1879–1955) and as Frye directs his readers, the motive for metaphor comes from "a desire to associate, and finally identify, the human mind with what goes on outside it."[23] In our technological age, we desire to associate our language of imagination with the language of our sciences such that they might converge on our language of practical aims, which, while repeating the lingua franca of modernity, can be understood for the pursuit of progress and power—for the construction of civilization.

Thus, the stories that have carried us here, to our technological present, have demanded not only an imaginative conformation but also a participatory response that has trained our gaze on nature to see it as raw material, awaiting agency to put it to work—to make it fit our imaginings, *to correlate what we see with what we imagine so we can make what we want* (as the story seems to go). Such stories organize our response to and handling of said material toward functionalist outcomes, discovering meaning only when materials are usable.

This brings me, finally, to two claims, among many, in Frye's lectures. First: "Literature does not reflect life, but it doesn't escape or withdraw from it either: *it swallows it*. And the imagination won't stop until it's swallowed everything. No matter what direction we start off in, the signposts of literature always keep pointing the same way, to a world where nothing is outside the human imagination."[24] Then this, returning us to the opening lecture: "[Imagination] is

23. Frye, *Educated Imagination*, 16.
24. Frye, *Educated Imagination*, 47–48 (emphasis added).

the power of constructing possible models of human experience. In the world of the imagination, anything goes that's imaginatively possible, but nothing really happens. If it did happen, it would move out of the world of imagination into the world of action."[25]

I find these claims apropos. They duly summarize my concerns, for they articulate what the principal stories of modernity have done. They have swallowed life, they have marshaled the imagination to act, creating a singular monologue of numbers to correlate observations with what we imagine, so we can produce what we want. The imaginative language of mathematics has liberated such language to move into the world of action. It has become an ethics: "Whatever does not conform to the rule of computation and utility is suspect."[26]

The result is the preeminence of the one narrative that contorts and constrains one's vision such that the lens of the technological imaginary has become the only way to see the world and this has shaped many of us into "bigots and fanatics."[27] Such persons are those no longer able to see their beliefs and actions as possibilities alongside others. Such persons close off the opportunity to imagine the world differently. They turn only to the language of mathematics, of computation and utility, to explain what they see, what they want, and what they do. Frye laments that for such persons, alongside those so enraptured by

25. Frye, *Educated Imagination*, 8.
26. Horkheimer and Adorno, *Dialectic of Enlightenment*, 6.
27. Frye, *Educated Imagination*, 46.

possibilities, by the limitlessness of imagination, action or decision is obstructed. But unlike the dilettante, bigots and fanatics are dangerous.

Perhaps Yuval Noah Harari's afterword in his *Sapiens* presents the danger well:

> Despite the astonishing things that humans are capable of doing, we remain unsure of our goals and we seem to be as discontented as ever. We have advanced from canoes to galleys to steam ships to space shuttles—but nobody knows where we are going. We are more powerful than ever before, but have very little idea what to do with all that power. Worse still, humans seem to be more irresponsible than ever. Self-made gods with only the laws of physics to keep us company, we are accountable to no one. We are consequently wreaking havoc on our fellow animals and on the surrounding ecosystem, seeking little more than our own comfort in amusement, yet never finding satisfaction.
>
> Is there anything more dangerous than dissatisfied and irresponsible gods who don't know what they want?[28]

Emerging from Babylon: A Humanizing Summons to Practice Dissent

Although provocative, I think Harari's final question above is not the right question. To be fair, Harari's point that such persons remain ignorant of ends might well correspond to Shannon Vallor's observation of persons beset by "*acute*

---

28. Yuval Noah Harari, *Sapiens: A Brief History of Humankind* (London: Vintage, 2011), 465–66.

technosocial opacity."[29] Vallor goes on to diagnose such blindness as the "increasingly difficult [capacity] to identify, seek, and secure the ultimate goal of ethics—a life worth choosing; a life lived *well*."[30] As the argument goes, acute technosocial opacity stonewalls perspective toward the good life and catches us up by the habits of the technological vision of life—standing reserves that supply a perpetual cache of resources to be used, and used up, or a persistent stream of data to be collated, assessed, and peddled for production or propaganda. Yet the narrative plot of techno-ontology guides our desires. We are trained to aspire toward more power and progress.

Accordingly, Harari's question falls short. We *do know* what we want: power and progress. The problem is that power and progress are not ends. They are, as stated in the first chapter, persistent as means. Desires are caught up by or bounded to such means. Techno-ontology narrates the end of ends, conforming desires toward power and progress as means to further power and progress, all the while cultivating discontent.

The *nature* we see is regularly outdone by the technological artifacts we and our machines engineer and the commodities they promise and proffer. Thus, the *nature* we have made becomes redundant to the *nature* we can develop. Upgrading everything becomes normative—because more power and more progress is the tail wagging the dog.

29. Vallor, *Technology and the Virtues*, 6.
30. Vallor, *Technology and the Virtues*, 6.

Modern human beings shaped by techno-ontology, there-fore, remain perpetually frustrated and deeply unfulfilled.[31]

Yet the frustration I am considering here reveals the inhumanity of demi-beings who have been torn apart by the prevailing ontology, left only with their will to power hugging nihilistic tendencies that anticipate violence. Transhumanists are indicative of this sort. Their manifesto offers a "negative perspective on human nature coupled with a technoscientific vision of how we should improve [progress]."[32] Apologists of transhumanism "confound emotionality with irrationality, dormant potential with stupidity, and disability with dispensability," while turning toward so-called technological resolutions to such *problems*. Such persons are dangerous.[33] Once again, their imagination has been conformed to know what they want: the means for more power and progress.

31. Sergei Bulgakov, for example, would regard such a state of being, the one unfulfilled, as a being moved toward nothingness. See Bulgakov, "Lamb of God: On the Divine Humanity (1933)," in *Sergii Bulgakov: Toward a Russian Political Theology*, ed. Rowan Williams (Edinburgh: T&T Clark, 1999), 163–228 (189–90).

32. Georg Franck, Sarah Spiekermann, Peter Hampson, Charles M. Ess, Johannes Hoff, and Mark Coeckelbergh, "Wider den Transhumanismus [Against transhumanism]," *Neue Zürcher Zeitung*, June 19, 2017, https://tinyurl.com/u8do4b4. Sarah Spiekermann speaks further about the blight of transhumanism and offers a link to her English translation of the *Neue Zürcher Zeitung* manifesto in "The Ghost of Transhumanism," The Privacy Surgeon, July 6, 2017, https://tinyurl.com/vlrjae4.

33. Spiekermann, "Ghost of Transhumanism."

Such persons are dangerous because they refuse to entertain new possibilities and find the status quo of the technological to be a mere inevitability—leaving satisfaction as a casualty of power and progress. The technological imaginary, or techno-ontology, coerces disdain and trains their gaze on manufactured probabilities. It turns human creativity toward hegemony. Rather, the technological imaginary tyrannizes human expectations for the *good* with promises of the *better*, which risks leaving human persons in a state of perpetual discontentment. In such a state of being, one will remain persistently unfulfilled.

Unfortunately, persons conformed by techno-ontology are often inoculated to see such malady. The pursuit of the better binds such persons to progress and to perpetual conquest. This is dangerous. Such persons are found "under the influence of that spirit of imposture," a power "given over to resentment," or disdain.[34] This is the coercive power of techno-ontology, which cultivates dissatisfaction in what is in and of nature, including human nature, as well as those means and materials of our own making. Accordingly, such persons might not be able to see, with due realism, the targeting and degrading of themselves and of particular others. They might overlook abuses of technology as mere accident or anomaly, reduced by a calculus that presents benefits as still outweighing costs. Moreover, impending risk might be relativized by the probabilities and the promise of future control.

Perhaps we too are such persons—persons contented in

34. Marcel, *Man against Mass Society*, 41, 55.

our state of being, as unfulfilled, which simply is a catalyst to search for the endless construction of means and the perpetual array of utility justifications for the administration of human agency in the building of Babylon.

If so, let Christ pray for us all: "Father, forgive them; for they do not know what they are doing" (Luke 23:34 NRSV).

But let us also hear the summons to leave Babylon: "Come out of her, my people, so that you do not take part in her sins, and so you do not take part in her plagues" (Rev 18:4 NRSV).

Perhaps such a prayer or summons will strike one as odd. To speak of idolatry, or sin, and the need for forgiveness in relation to the technological imaginary at this point might seem unnecessary. Perhaps it is hyperbolic, but I think it is also necessary.

This is my summons to dissent. As such, I think it apropos to give due attention to Stanley Hauerwas's contention that *the first task of the church is not to make the world more just but to make the world the world.*[35] So, our response to the summons, first, must be(come) a practice of dissent, of protest. William Stringfellow argues that "Christians are perpetually in the position of complaining about the status quo, whatever it

---

35. Stanley Hauerwas, "Where Would I Be without Friends," in *Faithfulness and Fortitude: In Conversation with the Theological Ethics of Stanley Hauerwas*, ed. Mark Nation (Edinburgh: T&T Clark, 2000), 313–32 (318). See also Hauerwas' reflections on this statement in his "How to Write a Theological Sentence," in *The Work of Theology* (Grand Rapids: Eerdmans, 2015), 122–46. Alternatively, read Hauerwas's "How to Write a Theological Sentence," ABC Religion and Ethics (September 26, 2013), https://tinyurl.com/y7ko3h9d.

happens to be."[36] This is not meant to be a slight—I do not mean to paint an image of people who whinge and whine out of contempt or belligerence. It is in being discipled by Christ that one comes to see the world *as the world.*

Dissent concerns a new seeing that Babylon is not Jerusalem, regardless of the "moral ultimacy in her destiny, her reputation, her capabilities, her authority, her glory." After all, "[the Christian's] insight and experience of reconciliation in Christ are such that no estate in secular society can possibly correspond to, or much approximate, the true society of which they are citizens in Christ. They are—everywhere, in every society—aliens. They are always, in any society, in protest."[37]

We should, therefore, learn to dissent of the modern mind, that is, the imaginative technological recasting of the world, which diminishes being to a state of nothingness, dissolving human agency, homogenizing human creativity, and leaving only a cacophony of functions to be exploited and expressed for the inauguration of more power and further progress. We must learn to dissent such a technological recasting (*mythos* or plot) of the world, where desires are cultivated by machine metaphors and where control over everything requires objectification.

We must learn to protest the technological age and the object of modern desire, power to power. We must learn to oppose the idolatry of the modern credo, "In technology we

36. William Stringfellow, *Dissenter in a Great Society* (Eugene, OR: Wipf & Stock, 2005), 162.
37. William Stringfellow, *An Ethic for Christians and Other Aliens in a Strange Land* (Eugene, OR: Wipf & Stock, 2004), 51, 162.

trust!" Furthermore, we must learn to oppose the bigotry and fanaticism that secures enthusiasm for modern achievements and the haughty conviction that it is *always* right to pursue technological answers to the problems of the technological civilization. We must learn to dispute the modern anthropology "that 'we are the people' and that 'wisdom was born with us.'"[38]

We must protest the narrative that has formed our technological civilization and present it as a worldly narrative, a narrative opposed to the world where we find ourselves.

The technological *mythos* is opposed to the possibility that we might wrestle against death in the midst of life, in the midst of struggle and suffering. Instead, it labors to flee from death by wielding and controlling it. As such, domination over the world has become normative in order to manufacture a heaven of our own making, which merely enslaves unfulfilled beings in an uncreative determining cycle of progress. It is governed by, as Barth puts it, an "absolute will for form, a will to which all the things we find existing about us are mere material to be moulded by man." In this way, all things are to be reduced to a harmony, although a harmony mediated by humanity's so-claimed and enacted godlikeness, for "[humanity] is almost capable of anything . . . [and] knows what is right!"[39]

But what is right? More power, of course. And power is progress.

---

38. Casserley, *Fate of Modern Culture*, 103.
39. Barth, "Man in the Eighteenth Century," 49, 27, 37.

Such a turn toward domination is the turn toward an egocentricity, toward the pursuit of self-affirmation, self-sufficiency, and self-satisfaction, toward the exalted ideal of the modern monad. This sequestered being "is an emanation, an image, a mirror of God himself," yet guided only by "its own most peculiar striving."[40] It is the striving of one given over to, conformed by, sin.

Such striving, then, is a mere striving toward nothingness, that *state* of being that remains unfulfilled and incomplete. We become disunited from the actuality of the world, including the actuality of the other; we learn to dislike the world as it is, while desiring a world of one's own making; and we quarrel with progress itself, like an addict given over to a drug, never satisfied or satiated. Yet as Berdyaev comments, "The egocentric always falls into the power of objectivization. Looking upon the world as an instrument for his service, the egocentric always ejects himself into the external world, and becomes dependent upon *it*."[41]

As such, our being remains in nothingness, stalled by sin, serving the coercive means (or gods) of power and progress while justifying our idolatry in the name of righting human injustice (the world ought not to be as it is).[42]

Of course, justice is narrated through the technological imaginary that sees frailty and finitude as injustices to

---

40. Barth, "Man in the Eighteenth Century," 64.
41. Berdyaev, *Slavery and Freedom*, trans. R. M. French (San Rafael, CA: Semantron Press, 2009), 133 (emphasis added).
42. For a brief discussion on sin, see Herbert McCabe, "A Long Sermon for Holy Week: Part 1, Holy Thursday: The Mystery of Unity," *New Blackfriars* 67, no. 788 (1986): 56–69 (59–60).

resolve. But death, or the fear of death, becomes the principal catalyst. Accordingly, as alluded to in the previous chapter, death reveals itself as a power to coerce human behavior as it is so often commissioned to justify the possibilities and promises of the technological future.

Let me explain with an anecdote: I stood in conversation with engineers, computer scientists, physicists, physicians, politicians, investors, and futurists at a recent event held over several days at a sprawling English estate. The purpose of the event was to gather a range of voices and expertise to think about the imminent confluence of genetic engineering and machine learning. But as I listened throughout the duration of the event, I often heard sentiments like the following: "We don't want persons to die or to suffer the fate of ignoble illnesses that seem senseless and cruel." "We desire health, and happiness, and security, and peace." "We should live on our own terms, as we choose, and to live for as long as possible." Genetic engineering and predictive competencies exaggerated through algorithms were presented as essential to secure such desires—and the technologies to make such expedient bioengineering possible were described as inevitable or already available.

But during a lively conversation with a computer scientist and a physicist late into the second evening, death was revealed as a sort of proof that the world *is* against us. Their respective death anxieties draped the objective reality of death with statements that expressed death as a disvalue, an unwanted reality, the greatest of harms. The backdrop was set for these individuals to draw on their imagination, which illuminated their desires, and the technologies in question were presented, among others, as the practical endeavors to actualize such desires. Both persons, therefore, presented the inevitability of death, as experienced now, as a problem to overcome by applied scientific and technological intervention. Research and development into thwarting death ought to be a principal aim, deserving abundant human and financial investment.

I dissented.

Both persons were dismayed at my protest. I opposed the desire to continue extending life as a rule of power and progress. I disputed the justifications for such investment all the while persons, human beings in our society, and around the world, remain abandoned to loneliness, isolation, exclusion, impoverishment, and other dehumanizing conditions.[43] I dissented their preoccupations with biological death and possible technological remediations, while they failed to see that death takes on many forms in this world, even while persons are alive—forms of death that do not need a technological solution. But they would not relent: their hypothetical scenarios intended to persuade me of the utility and necessity of these emerging technologies to control the timing and experience of death, to overcome death, and to manufacture biological life by design, by desire, became increasingly impassioned. They were concerned, ultimately, with nothing else but death and control. Their subsequent arguments and illustrations merely revealed the magnitude of their anxieties and their conformation by techno-ontology. Their intentions to flee from death merely

43. Stringfellow, *Ethic for Christians*, 68–70.

illumined its moral power, which habituates the turn toward technological controls.

As to their response to human loneliness: without pause, they advocated for the continued development into compassionate-care robots and value-sensitive social algorithms, which might not only meet the basic needs of isolated persons but also respond appropriately to human emotions or sensibilities.

Their pictures painted, their scenarios scripted, their desires displayed a fear of death and a total trust in technology. Death was portrayed as the epitome of hostile nature and seemed to determine everything, every decision. But their unwitting presentation of death as a moral power was exactly correct. Death as a power complicit in the shaping of our modern imagination, therefore, had turned their gaze on technology as the probable route of escape from fate and finitude. They have been trained accordingly.

My response, a frustrating riposte to their apology for technology, was this: although I think improving the lives of persons is a good thing, and extending life can be one of these goods, I desire for people to live and to die well. I desire for people to live and to die in hope, such that each of us might live humanly. To delay death, as they expressed, would not help us to do that. It would simply habituate frustration and dissatisfaction, for a technology that might delay death by ten years, by the discontent conditioned through techno-ontology, will not be sufficient. Rather, people will, by way of a trust in technique, by a desire for control and the continued fear of death, seek the next technological advance that will delay death even longer. Twenty years. Fifty years.

One hundred years. Yet, as I argued above, each one will perpetually remain unfulfilled and discontented.

My question to them was this: How does the turn toward technological rationalities and interventions adequately prepare us for suffering, for tragedy, for death?

"It doesn't," the physicist responded, with refreshing candor. "But it will save us from such shit!" he exclaimed.

One might chuckle at his exclamation, given the irony expressed by Ernest Becker (1924–1974):

> As [Michel de] Montaigne [1533–92] put it, on the highest throne in the world man sits on his arse. Usually this epigram makes people laugh. . . . But if we push the observation even further and say men sit not only on their arse, but also over a warm and fuming pile of their own excrement—the joke is no longer funny. . . . The anus and its incomprehensible, repulsive product represents not only physical determinism and boundness but the fate as well of all that is physical: decay and death. . . . The upsetting thing about anality is that it reveals that all culture, all man's creative life-ways, are in some basic part of them a fabricated protest against natural reality, a denial of the truth of the human condition, and an attempt to forget the pathetic creature that man is.[44]

Another might also assess such a phrase as idolatrous. But I think such an exclamation is to be expected. This is the rhetoric of the world—we will know everything (Gen 3:5). This is as the grammar of sin, of the fall.

It is a phrase expected of those who have not learned to hasten patience. Such patience is a faithful waiting on the

44. Ernest Becker, *The Denial of Death* (New York: Free Press, 1973), 31–33.

good providence of God to answer our questions about the world, so full of tragedy and trial. After all, "the kind of training" that the Christian has been called to practice "has everything to do with death." As Hauerwas rightly summarizes, "To follow Jesus is to go with him to Jerusalem where he will be crucified. To follow Jesus, therefore, is to undergo a training that refuses to let death, even death at the hands of enemies, determine the shape of our living."[45]

In a world that cultivates haste for progress and power, governed by the liturgies and linear time of operating-system inaugurations and iPhone unveilings, where many proclaim "In technology we trust!" we need to learn to say something of "God," as Stanley Hauerwas might acclaim.

And by *we*, I mean Christians.

But we often don't.

Instead, our language is similar to that of the technological world. After all, the ubiquity of technology makes our study within and conformation by its schooling most probable. But it might also be a malignant legacy of post-Reformation theologies.[46] As Craig Gay comments, "Enthusiasm for disciplined empirical reasoning in the practical reform of material life was, for example, one of the distinctive features of 17th century English Protestant culture." Post-Reformation theologies also bolstered commitment to early modern scientific endeavors, including aims to conquer nature through practical interventions so as to reclaim,

45. Stanley Hauerwas, *Working with Words: On Learning to Speak Christian* (Eugene, OR: Cascade Books, 2011), 78.
46. Craig Gay, *The Way of the (Modern) World: Or, Why It's Tempting to Live as If God Doesn't Exist* (Grand Rapids: Eerdmans, 1998).

or to move toward, the new Jerusalem—"to 're-engineer' both the church and the world."[47]

The impetus to reshape nature by human hands and technological interventions in post-Reformation theologies was concerned with human liberation or freedom. Gay also observes, drawing on his reading of George Grant's essay "In Defense of North America," that "the practical conquest of nature eventually ceased to be understood as a religious duty. . . . And in the absence of [explicit] religious understanding, a kind of nihilism [began] to surface . . . [becoming] a hegemonic cultural force." Such a cultural force, Gay continues, is "pursued with a kind of quasi-religious intensity. For it has come to be believed that modern technological development will eventually give rise to a kind of rationalized 'kingdom of man.'"[48] The modern impetus to continue this pursuit, a pursuit of the antichrist, continues with said intensity. Modern humanity continues to consider that "what they are doing" is concerned not with sin or idolatry but "with the liberation [salvation] of mankind."[49]

---

47. Craig Gay, *Modern Technology and the Human Future: A Christian Appraisal* (Downers Grove, IL: IVP Academic, 2018), 106, 108–9. Georg Franck and his colleagues write concerning transhumanism: "This perspective is best recognized by a superstitious belief in science [and technology] as saviour and a distanced contempt for our human nature: our fragility, our mortality, our sentience, our self-awareness, and our embodied sense of 'who' we are (as distinct from a 'what')" (Spiekermann, "Ghost of Transhumanism").
48. Gay, *Modern Technology*, 109. See Grant's essay "In Defense of North America," in *Technology and Empire*, in *Collected Works of George Grant*, 3:480–503.
49. Gay, *Modern Technology*, 110.

All that is needed, so the argument often goes, is a constellation of propositions and principles to guide human action and to ensure values outweigh disvalues, benefits outnumber costs. Such principles can come in the form of a few "secular" imperatives, such as those offered by futurist and World Health Organization expert adviser on human genome editing Jamie Metzl.[50] Or they can be regarded as essential equipment for churchgoers in a technological age, as offered by the signatories of the Ethics and Religious Liberty Commission's statement on "Artificial Intelligence: An Evangelical Statement of Principles."[51]

But the sciences taken up and the technologies deployed in the liberation of humankind are not exempt from the fall. The admonition of and rational assent to principles is inadequate to protest the conformation that has occurred by the ontology of our age, with its "fantastic attitude that technical capability ought to be implemented just because it exists, without regard to the moral character [shaped by it]." Such an attitude is not only naive but also foolish. Perhaps such folly is expected, given that "technology and the political implementation of technology as technocracy" is the hallmark of a dark age, as Stringfellow laments.[52]

50. Jamie Metzl, "Human Gene Editing Is Too Transformative to Be Guided by the Few," *Financial Times*, March 18, 2019, https://tinyurl.com/wz8hjn9.

51. Ethics and Religious Liberty Commission, "Artificial Intelligence: An Evangelical Statement of Principles," April 11, 2019, https://tinyurl.com/y6p57knr.

52. William Stringfellow, *The Politics of Spirituality* (Philadelphia: Westminster, 1984), 73, 71.

By "dark age," Stringfellow means to describe the reality of postindustrial technocratic societies where "the power of death is pervasive and militant and in which people exist without hope or else in pursuit of transient, fraudulent, or delusive hopes."[53] As I said above, it is a period of perpetual dissatisfaction and unrelenting disillusionment—the only hope is a functional hoping for perpetual control. The commodities of such control, however, are often fleeting or futile, contributing to the malaise of the modern technological society.

This is the reality we ought to protest.

In the modern pursuit of certainty and control, in the demonic quest of Adam to secure knowledge of everything, of good and evil, we have been adulterated by folly and conformed to the image of the machine. Now, bolstered by the triumphs of technique, we labor to construct our world—shaping all *things* as we desire.[54] Protest, therefore, is right: "in resistance persons live most humanly."[55] Dissenting from techno-ontology is humanizing.

53. Stringfellow, *Politics of Spirituality*, 69.
54. George Grant, "Man-Made Man," in *Collected Works of George Grant*, vol. 3, 255–70.
55. Stringfellow, *Ethic for Christians*, 156.

5

———

Saying, Seeing, Becoming Human

Human beings cannot be thought of merely as an assortment
of objects. Human beings are subjects, too. Human beings
are given to be before God and in relation to, with, and for
other human beings (and to the entire cosmos, for that matter). A human being, as though a mere object, turned into
a tool and organized for impersonal usage, is not a human
being at all.[1] Neither is one a human being when trapped by
an endless search for more power that trains a state of discontentment not only for the present but also in progress.

Here is the point of concern. Here is the locus of the crisis.

1. Berdyaev, "Spiritual Condition of the Modern World," 66.

The crisis of techno-ontology, as sketched, is not a technological crisis but an anthropological crisis. The crisis is the turning point at which we either participate in human becoming or persist toward nothingness—that state of being that remains unfulfilled. Either way, being (whether fulfilled or unfulfilled) demands performative attention. That is to suggest human life is constituted and oriented by, performed out of, the stories we learn from the communities to which we belong.[2] Being is constituted within such locations of moral meaning expressed in the various social practices and narrative traditions; it is constituted even as such narratives are interrupted, interrogated, and revised in relation and response to the peculiarities of nature. Because nothingness remains a part, or state, of being contingent on performative attention, even in the direst of "unhuman" states, of the most bureaucratized, objectivized, mechanized, and atomized states of being, one might begin toward the fulfillment of being human.

For Julian Casserley (1909–1978), reflecting his Thomism, there is no *might* about it: "Human nature *will* insist on being human," even if persons are caught up by the idolatry of technology and its heterodox ontology for a time.[3] I am not as optimistic as Casserley seems to be. But his sentiment might offer us a motive expectation that condescends even to the deepest abyss of nothingness adorned by the determining powers or enframing impulses of techno-ontology.

2. Stanley Hauerwas, *Vision and Virtue* (Notre Dame: University of Notre Dame Press, 1981), 68–89; Hauerwas, *Community of Character* (Notre Dame: University of Notre Dame Press, 1981), 111–28.
3. Casserley, *Fate of Modern Culture*, 75 (emphasis added).

Perhaps this proclamation of becoming human resources a particular kind of hope for the crisis at hand. Yet one must not remain satisfied with the *state* of being, for *it is* the problem that technology raises and occludes all at once. Technology as an ontology offers a different vision of human being caught up and determined by the schema of reason, autonomy of will, and power of technique. But such a human being is no human being fulfilled at all.

So it is especially important to hear the warning that Nicholas Berdyaev presented nearly ninety years ago: "The problem of our time is the problem of man, the salvation of the human person from corruption, the vocation and purpose of man, the resolution of basic issues of society and culture in the light of the Christian idea about being [becoming] human."[4]

But resolution for those conformed, deformed, and determined by techno-ontology, unfulfilled in their state of being, is not to be resolved by the prompt administration of a technological artifact or the commodities such an artifact might produce. Rather, such a determinative turn toward technological rationality would merely reinforce nothingness. The response must be(come) a sustained performance as we learn to struggle together toward human flourishing in the ambiguities of the present. Thus, the resolution *is* the human task. That is to say, to put it plainly, Berdyaev is right: the answer for our contemporary crisis is to be found in our participation in human becoming. As such, "The truth must be

4. Berdyaev, "Spiritual Condition of the Modern World," 68.

practiced in life."[5] Such practices are to be taught and to be lived out as humanizing actions that emphasize and validate the reality and condition of human life "in the very midst of the conflict, distortion, alienation, disorientation, chaos, [and] decadence of the Fall."[6] They are to be lived out both before God and for our fellows.

Such humanizing actions are what I mean by the art of living, the way for one's becoming, development, and fulfillment. The way of living toward human being is not to be groomed by "confused thought and invalid aspiration," which is sure to make of our being a "shapeless ruin."[7] The way, of course a way of discipleship, the way of Jerusalem in the midst of Babylon, demands that we must remain with Christ such that we might be schooled in the art of living *for* our technological age.

Performative Attention toward Human Flourishing

Such an idea, a training that enables being as such, might be well served by the ancient concept of *paideia*. Although it is a concept that cannot be domesticated well by modern euphemisms, it remains important. In part, it understands human being in ways that correspond with my concern for the long-suffering formation of the human person con-

5. Berdyaev, "Spiritual Condition of the Modern World," 68.
6. Stringfellow, *Ethic for Christians*, 55.
7. Casserley, *Fate of Modern Culture*, 76, 111.

fronted and conformed by the repetitions and remembering of stories.

Indeed, the *paideia* by which our character is shaped, or our being becomes, is trained both by suffering the actualities of life and by education. As John Behr has commented on several occasions, the dialectic of suffering and education can be drawn from the ancients, who saw suffering, or experience, as the way we learn. Yet education is needed "to make suffering—the common fate of [us all]—into the creative process by which we become human."[8] Paradoxically, for Simone Weil, this creative process is the *decreation* of false divinities and the long labor toward a nothingness fulfilled by the God who renounces being everything so that we might renounce being something (i.e., the man-God of our modern imagination).[9] Such a nothingness is not fettered by discontent but freed for both God and neighbor—thus freed toward humanity.

Returning to the ideal of Greek culture, *paideia* is also assumed and affirmed by several early Christian fathers, including Origen (c. 184–253) and Clement (c. 150–215).[10]

8. John Behr, "Christian Humanism: The Beginning of Christian *Paideia*," in *Re-envisioning Christian Humanism: Education and the Restoration of Humanity*, ed. Jens Zimmermann (Oxford: Oxford University Press, 2016), 23–27. See also Behr, *Becoming Human: Meditations on Christian Anthropology in Word and Image* (Crestwood, NY: St. Vladimir's Seminary Press, 2013); Behr, *The Mystery of Christ: Life in Death* (Crestwood, NY: St. Vladimir's Seminary Press, 2006).

9. Simone Weil, *Gravity and Grace*, trans. Emma Crawford and Mario von der Ruhr (New York: Routledge, 2002).

10. See Frances M. Young, "Towards a Christian *Paideia*," in *The Cambridge History of Christianity*, ed. Margaret Mitchell and Frances M. Young

The three Cappadocians also see *paideia*, because of their own experience and education, as the way of becoming a human being. They regard *paideia* as formative, and the classical material for learning is beneficial. Yet one has also to learn to be discerning—to be as the bees. Basil (330–379) presents the apian imagery in his *Address to Young Men* to remind his young readers that discrimination of both good and bad texts is also to be learned. Although Basil regards it wise to gather wisdom from any source available, one must beware the poisons. Christians, therefore, must learn to harvest the blooms of flowers on thorny stems as with the bees, who "neither approach all flowers equally, nor in truth do they attempt to carry off entire those upon which they alight, but taking only so much of them as is suitable for their work, they suffer the rest to go untouched. We ourselves too, if we are wise, having appropriated from this literature what is suitable to us and akin to the truth, will pass over the remainder."[11]

Finding benefit in Greek literature, and therefore culture, is not sufficient, however. Such *paideia* is not the principal telos. Rather, the early Christian fathers are concerned with what the Scriptures teach, with how the prophets and apos-

(Cambridge: Cambridge University Press, 2006), 484–500; Jelle Wytzes, "Paideia and Pronoia in the Works of Clemens Alexandrinus," *Vigiliae Christianae* 9 (1955): 148–58; Wytzes, "The Twofold Way: Platonic Influences in the Work of Clement of Alexandria," *Vigiliae Christianae* 11 (1957): 226–45.

11. Basil, *On Greek Literature*, trans. Roy J. Deferrari and Martin R. P. McGuire, Loeb Classical Library 270 (London: William Heinemann; Cambridge, MA: Harvard University Press, 1934), 377–435, here 391, https://tinyurl.com/ozntgob.

tles, for example, educate us. The law and the gospel, if you will, is understood as *paideutic*. Gregory of Nyssa (335–394), for example, regards Christ as the chief pedagogue, "as 'the educator' of [hu]mankind," in whom and by whom we are to become as he is—to return to God and to become human.[12] Accordingly, we are invited to heed *his* words, and the words of those human beings who are the instruments of his Spirit, and to give due attention to the way.[13]

This distinction between Greek and Christian *paideia* by Basil is not to be missed. He is cognizant that there are possibly many pedagogues in one's life, shaping and contouring life accordingly. The corresponding cultures, if you will, might be held in tension—and productively so, where one completes the other (as one might see in climbing John Climacus's ladder and his account of Greek virtue ethics completed by a Christian telos and the corresponding habits).[14] However, as Gregory realizes, for those tutored between two cultures where tension is broken or threatened, decisions concerning such *paideutic* influences must be made.[15] Dissent, as previously summoned, is as a revolt against a *paideutic* influence discerned to be a dead anchor, pulling on another toward the depths of corruption and callousness.

---

12. Werner Jaeger, *Early Christianity and Greek Paideia* (Cambridge, MA: Belknap, 1961), 133n29, 98–100.
13. Jaeger, *Early Christianity and Greek Paideia*, 92–95.
14. See John Climacus, *The Ladder of Divine Ascent* (Mahwah, NJ: Paulist, 1982).
15. To this point of wrestling with various educational models and subsequent decision, see also Jennifer Herdt's brief discussion of Augustine and the *paideia* tradition of education in *Putting on Virtues: The Legacy of Splendid Vices* (Chicago: University of Chicago Press, 2008), 64–65.

That is to say, dissent is to be regarded a material social performance, an art where discernment and protest are practiced to expose and rebuke fallen powers and principalities such that human life might be nurtured and fulfillment of all life might be actualized. The target of such dissent is not the innate conditions of existence, but rather in what humans have invented—or imagined and brought to bear. Its target is a terrible inheritance, a ubiquitous narrative with a clandestine *dys–paideia*, which does not liberate us but encloses us within a cave, a civilization, of our making. As Donald MacKinnon (1913–1994) comments, speaking of coercive powers hewn from our own hands and drawing from Plato's imagery, we are thus left "alienated from ourselves, seeing only our shadows."[16]

Dissent thus serves to remind us that we are not to be people storied by the victories of modern science and the merits of technology; we are not to turn our gaze toward a "Kingdom of Man"[17] that exhausts itself in the reciprocal pursuit of means caught between sin and fate. Some will recognize such bondage for what it is; they will realize their captivity and conformation toward nothingness, dissent and turn toward liberation and the riddle of becoming a human being. They will follow in the steps of Moses and of Gregory of Nyssa, who draws a parallel between Moses's life and his own, in which he avoided applying himself to profane study because of the care of his sister Macrina to educate him in

16. Donald M. MacKinnon, "Christology and Protest (1988)," in *Philosophy and the Burden of Theological Honesty*, ed. John C. McDowell (London: T&T Clark, 2011), 265–76 (270).

17. Casserley, *Fate of Modern Culture*, 76.

the sublime ideal.[18] That is to say, while contemplating the contrasting *paideia* of Moses, both his training at the feet of the Egyptians *and* at the feet of his biological mother, Gregory discovered his own reflection. As such, when conflict arose between persons representing the two cultures that were conforming Moses, Moses chose to turn toward his mother's *paideia*, killing the icon of profane education. This too was Gregory's choice when confronted by profane doctrines, which "strive to appear stronger than the word of Israel." He realizes: "Truly sterile is profane education: it is always in labor but never bears a child."[19]

But dissent does not guarantee commitment to such liberation, as above. It does not guarantee relief from such labor pains. Such freedom and relief are not to be thought as commodities wrought by the strength of absolute will. Freedom and relief are not efficient commodities of modern technique. Rather, they come by suffering and education, and they open us up to the world and its "wildness [that] lies in wait," as G. K. Chesterton (1874–1936) puts it.[20] Since dissent does not guarantee such things, the allure of profane education can remain a catalyst for one's malignant conformation. MacKinnon, continuing to reflect on the words of both Socrates and Jesus, offers further perspective: "Before we were freed, we did not recognize our bondage for what

18. Gregory of Nyssa, *The Life of St. Macrina*, trans. W. K. Lowther Clarke (London: Society for Promoting Christian Knowledge, 1916), 36–38.
19. Gregory of Nyssa, *The Life of Moses*, trans. Abraham J. Malherbe and Everett Ferguson (New York: Paulist, 1973), 1.18, 2.13, 2.11, pp. 34, 57–58.
20. G. K. Chesterton, *Orthodoxy* (San Francisco: Ignatius, 1995), 87.

it was. But now we know, and if we seek to return in fear of freedom, we do so disillusioned and despairing, preferring a security [over the riddle] in which we no longer believe to the unknown and unfamiliar."[21] MacKinnon concludes this reflection by citing the Gospel according to Matthew: "Let the dead bury their own dead" (Matt 8:22). "Take up [your] cross and follow me" (Matt 16:24).

What might such words mean in our present context?

They mean that the summons to dissent cannot be the only summons. Rather, the radical witness to which we are called, the invitation to be discipled at the feet of Christ, to be schooled on the way to Jerusalem, both from and to Galilee, is, as MacKinnon writes, a calling to be "fashioned after the model of the 'good shepherd.' It is no generalized caring, but a strenuous, if always imperfect and mutilated, fidelity to the way of Jesus."[22] The witness of the Christian, of the church in the world and for the world, is not complete with mere dissent. While dissent might remind us that we are not to make the world more just but are to make the world the world (let the dead bury the dead), it does not illustrate a complete picture of the world that we are to learn to say, and therefore to see. We must, as the summon continues, endure to follow after Jesus (take up your cross and follow me).

As a way of enduring *education*, Christian *paideia*, therefore, must be an investment in such suffering and learning. It must be an investment in *the way*, by which we come to

21. MacKinnon, "Christology and Protest," 270.
22. MacKinnon, "Christology and Protest," 275.

learn to say (therefore see) the world as Christ does. The investment is realized by the revelation of reality through human becoming and by the actualization of the narrative vision in the world. "In other words," as Hauerwas argues, "the enterprise of Christian ethics primarily helps us to see. We can only act within the world we can envision, and we can envision the world rightly only as we are trained to see. We do not come to see merely by looking, but must develop disciplined skills through initiation into that community that attempts to live faithful to the story of God."[23] Accordingly, Hauerwas asserts: "To learn to follow Jesus is the training necessary to become a human being. To be a human being is not a natural condition, but requires training."[24]

Such *paideia*, therefore Christian *paideia*, is not to be considered as a spontaneous fiat. It requires sustained attention, or "constant care."[25] The dialectic of suffering and learning must be cultivated such that a *state* of being that remains unfulfilled and incomplete might not persist.

Accordingly, *paideia* requires, at the very least, two essential elements: first, it requires the guiding of one's gaze on a living, and therefore plastic, ideal. By *plastic* it must be understood that the "ideal of human character which [the ancients] wished to educate each individual to attain was not an empty abstract pattern, existing outside time and

23. Hauerwas, *Peaceable Kingdom*, 29–30.
24. Hauerwas, *Working with Words*, 78.
25. Jaeger, *Early Christianity and Greek Paideia*, 86.

space. It was the living ideal . . . [never] fixed and final."[26] In this way, character remains open to the evolutions of individual, communal, and cultural flourishing. *Paideia*, therefore, has no idealized end, no definitive solution. *Paideutic* practice considers the "object of learning [that] plays the part of the mold by which the subject is shaped."[27]

Literature provides such a mold. That is to say, for the ancients, literature was *paideia*. In it and by it, one was formed. In it and by it, culture was shaped. To be sure, such literature was disseminated by the learned pedagogue, or teacher, who taught literature through recitation and imitation. The same can be said of Christian *paideia*, which saw the words of the Scriptures and the words of proclamation, as powerfully conforming: "It is with his words that a teacher teaches and a spiritual guide guides, words which are demonstrated to be trustworthy by the manner of life of the speaker, yet words which also persuade us of his trustworthiness."[28]

By such an encounter with words, with the imagination illumined by words, by narrative both recited and lived, the *paideia* is the way that humans can be transformed.

But the second critical element is time. Consider a corollary term to *paideia*, *discipline*. Human beings are conformed by discipline—by the shaping of human being over time. Discipline comes not by fits and starts but through a labor of longsuffering. As Rowan Williams puts it, "Being a 'dis-

26. Werner Jaeger, *Paideia: The Ideals of Greek Culture*, vol. 1, *Archaic Greece: The Mind of Athens* (Oxford: Oxford University Press, 1986), xxiv.
27. Jaeger, *Early Christianity and Greek Paideia*, 91.
28. Behr, "Christian Humanism," 30.

ciple,' a learner, in that sense is a state of being in which you are looking and listening without interruption." Accordingly, "Disciples watch, they remain alert, attentive, watching symbolic acts as well as listening for instructive words; watching the actions that give the clue to how reality is being reorganized." Disciples, therefore, remain attentive both to life and to literature, to suffering and to learning, so that the way in which one not only sees but also experiences the world is transformed. "The disciple is where he or she is in order to be changed; so that the way in which he or she sees and experiences the whole world changes."[29]

Time is not merely consecutive. *Paideutic* discipline reimagines time, shaping disciples accordingly. Williams discusses time poignantly:

> How religious communities spend their time is a serious and central theme. Time is not undifferentiated; its passage is marked in ways that are thought to be significant. So the passage of time becomes not just a trajectory of acquisition (acquiring property, acquiring power, acquiring security); it comes to be about the repeated accumulation, as you might say, of meaning, returning to symbolic resources to rediscover aspects of the universe you inhabit. Aspects of yourself; to reconnect specific ongoing experiences with steady, regular or rhythmical patterns, laid out in the language and practice of a religious community. You keep going back to the practices, the stories, in celebration and commemoration. Time, therefore, becomes neither simply cyclical nor simply linear. It moves, you change; at the same time there is something to which you *return*, to rediscover and enlarge the understanding

29. Rowan Williams, *Being Disciples: Essentials of the Christian Life* (London: SPCK, 2016), 2–3, 6–7.

acquired in the passage of time. And all of that adds up to dissolving any idea that time is a limited commodity (or indeed any kind of commodity) that has to be squeezed as hard as possible in order to keep the trajectory of acquisition going. Time is a complex and rich gift; it is the medium in which we not only grow and move forward but also constructively return and resource—literally re-source—ourselves.[30]

Such reimagination of time collapses past and future on the present, claiming the disciple's state of being, pronouncing a judgement on it, and summoning attention toward human history. *Paideutic* discipline both protests the malady of humanity and affirms the truth of human being. Reimagination of time means that we must read, reread, and read again the words of the pedagogue, to stay in such time that marches forward in circles, to encounter the one who refuses to let us turn our backs on human being, both ours and others, and who resources the strength for interrogation and transformation in the world we have been given and the world we encounter.

Training, therefore, is an interruption to the inhumanity of the status quo. It is humanizing.

We must, therefore, follow Christ to Jerusalem. Jerusalem, as with the road from and to Galilee, reveals a narrative history of Christ, one that disciplines the "Christian imagination and its resultant performance." "Follow me" is as a teacher's summons reordered by the medium of time, where we move forward and return to his words and his steps,

30. Rowan Williams, *Being Human: Bodies, Minds, Persons* (London: SPCK, 2018), 77–78.

which re-sources ourselves "in the ontological depth that the kenotic form of God in Christ expresses."[31]

This is a narrative history where the terribleness and the paradox of the gospel are confronted, and often evaded, only to be confronted again with the interrogating discipline of time reordered. As I have written elsewhere, reflecting on MacKinnon's essays *God the Living and True* (1940) and his *The Church of God* (1940),

> Apart from Jesus Christ, we cannot know who it is we are (and before whom we are gathered). With the coming of Christ, however, we can know in his *illic et tunc* [there and then] as well as in his *hic et nunc* [here and now] that we are sinners reconciled to God, Father, Son, and Holy Spirit. [Yet we] come to distress of "the terrible tale of Christ's coming and rejection" as with the paradox of the church (the gathering by Christ of those who have crucified him), which "is only resolved when we have grasped . . . the primacy of the divine initiative."[32]

The divine initiative is the kenotic performance of the Son, who submits himself "to the very substance of human life, in its inexorable finitude, in its precarious ambiguity, in its

---

31. John C. McDowell, "Donald MacKinnon, Speaking Honestly to Ecclesial Power," in *Kenotic Ecclesiology: Select Writing of Donald MacKinnon*, ed. John C. McDowell, Scott A. Kirkland, and Ashley John Moyse (Minneapolis: Fortress Press, 2016), 1–30 (24).

32. Ashley John Moyse, "The Terrible Occasion and Particular Paradox of the Gospel," in *Kenotic Ecclesiology*, 33–40 (34).

movement to despair."[33] Commenting on MacKinnon's argument, John C. McDowell writes,

> What is meant by God and the qualities predicated of God, such as omnipotence, are transformed. The political consequences of such an account of theological discipline are pronounced. [Any vision] of divine potency is subverted in favor of understanding the truth of power itself to demand keeping company with the Crucified. It is his life that shapes what is meant not only by divine power, but its proper reflection on human performance.[34]

Our human performance is shaped as we stay with him in his descent, to the tomb, where all our hopes are set[35]—where we are educated not to labor for our own salvation against death, and where we experience a kenotic reality that is true, and beautiful, and good. It is a reality that endures despair, unlike the world of our making.

Endurance, however, is not a summons to masochism or to futility. It is a summons to labor *through* despair such that one might suffer, learn, and practice the principal virtues that lead to the possibility of an ethical life—a life fulfilled. Such a life is one that discovers, through despair but not because of it, the possibilities that arise from a right saying and seeing of the world—a saying and seeing that renders

33. Donald MacKinnon, "Reflections on Donald Baillie's Treatment of the Atonement," in *Christ, Church, and Society: Essays on John Baillie and Donald Baillie*, ed. David Ferguson (Edinburgh: T&T Clark, 1993), 115–21 (115).
34. McDowell, "MacKinnon, Speaking Honestly," 25.
35. Donald M. MacKinnon, "The Tomb Was Empty (1946)," in McDowell, *Philosophy and the Burden*, 255–60.

persons as primary, that cultivates being that remains ever present and faithful toward one's fellow creatures (toward intersubjectivity, as Gabriel Marcel would say).[36] To be sure, possibilities might also include the proper attachment and use of technological artifacts, which are governed by creative intersubjectivity (whether as charity or attachment, or likely both in convergence). In fact, priority of being can adequately discipline technology to the service of human becoming.

However, as a *dys-paideia*, a profane doctrine, techno-ontology directs us to spend time learning from machine metaphors and to participate in efficient causes. It disciplines our attention toward conventional categories of power and the moral adjudication of utility. The profane doctrine of modern culture promises us freedom *from* dependence, from intersubjectivity. It promises relief *from* the human condition. It promises power fashioned *from* the objective resources and information progressively gathered, ordered, and put to labor for one's benefit. It promises control *over* nature, including human nature. In essence, techno-ontology refuses the kenotic reorientation and flees from despair, anticipating violence, eventually turning against each other and ourselves.[37] It betrays the truth of both divine and human being.

The art of living, a euphemism for Christian *paideia*, is a training to live humanly in and for the fallen world. It is

---

36. Gabriel Marcel, *The Mystery of Being*, vol. 2, *Faith and Reality* (South Bend, IN: St. Augustine's, 1951), 1–17.

37. Gabriel Marcel, *Homo Viator: Introduction to a Metaphysic of Hope*, trans. Emma Craufurd (Chicago: Henry Regnery, 1951), 37–38.

a training that interrogates and transforms, such that one might learn to live humanly for our technological age.

The Art of Living for the Technological Age

The art of living, therefore, is a material-social practice that conforms being such that the good takes on flesh and goads human beings toward human flourishing. Such goading, or social practices, evokes a sense of movement in the worlds we encounter. Our movements have little to do with assent to principles or dogmatic execution of tasks and more to do with a learning to navigate the world and its complexities, its particularities moment by moment, as a human being. Being, as such, is thus cultivated by the habits one practices, or the postures one simulates, and these habits remind us what human beings are.

Shannon Vallor has looked to the habits of virtues, broadly considered, to remind us who we are in her *Technology and the Virtues.* Her project is a reminder that well-being is a becoming nurtured by habituation. For Vallor, the virtues might inform and instruct the social milieu, where persons must learn to struggle toward the life well lived, which is also a struggling together with others who may have failed "to jointly and wisely deliberate about the collective impact of their actions."[38] She thus introduces twelve technosocial virtues, informed by a range of virtue traditions, which included self-control, humility, empathy, and courage, among others considered essential for learning to

38. Vallor, *Technology and the Virtues*, 53.

navigate a challenging technological present, an uncertain technological future, and the many other persons gathered.[39]

Surely her work here reminds us that the virtue traditions have a long history of resourcing people to face the world without fear and with the expectation for wisdom. Unfortunately, one might question whether Vallor does well to understand the ontological significance of virtue as it relates to technology. It may be that she too falls prey to the technological imagination that considers everything as a resource to be used to accomplish one's aim—in this case, the administration of virtues for navigating the technological present and uncertain future. For Vallor, the virtues cultivated from Aristotle to Confucius to Buddha are mere resources, with which one must determine their respective utility (or "purchase") and "reactivate" to accomplish one's self-determination.[40] The assumption is that we should use what is of benefit and discard the remainder. In her words: "We ask what conceptual and practical resources they *can* provide for the journey we need to make from our contemporary condition toward the good life for *us*, where 'us' refers to the increasingly interdependent techno-moral community now being constituted on a global scale."[41]

Although conversant with the virtues and the traditions, Vallor turns back to the sort of grammar incumbent to our technological conformation. She loses a sense of categorical

39. Vallor, *Technology and the Virtues*, 120.
40. Vallor, *Technology and the Virtues*, 63–64.
41. Vallor, *Technology and the Virtues*, 64.

difference between *paideia* and programs, which reflect ancient and modern educational modalities. One is left wondering whether her project understands the longsuffering and education of the virtue tradition, which demands one's self to be conformed accordingly (even across several traditions), only thereafter discerning poison from promise as discussed above. I am left wondering whether her selection of such virtues is a result of "lazy contemplation [and] overweening pride" or "long search [and] true judgment."[42] The difference is significant, as Jonathan Swift (1667–1745) would argue: the former leaves one with the spider's modern remnants, flybane and cobwebs, while the latter offers the bee's ancient gifts, honey and wax.

One might go in circles trying to determine whether Vallor's project is a spider or a bee, but it should be stressed that her attention to the challenges introduced by the ontology of our age is apropos. Moreover, her concern that persons are blinded to understand the *good* uses of technological artifacts because of technologies conforming habits echoes my concerns. She wants to know "how our moral habits can be made sufficiently *flexible* and responsive to emerging and unanticipated techno-social developments." Accordingly, she too has turned toward "moral habilitation," to the conformation of being, which might resource a way forward—a way to "engender greater *self-control* and discipline, such that we, and not our technologies, become the authors of

---

42. Jonathan Swift, "The Battle of the Books," in *The Works of Jonathan Swift* (New York: P. O'Shea, 1865), 2:367–90, here 376.

our habits and desires."[43] Her call toward flexibility also echoes a sense that such virtues are not as reified principles to be wielded, as cogs in a moral machinery, and positioned against our technological age. Instead, they are to shape our being such that we might be able to see the essential nature of things and learn to struggle toward human flourishing, even while laboring to exercise our creativity, ingenuity, and industry.

Yet I cannot help but see Vallor's project as one that aims to make the world more just by seeking to resource the self to navigate the technological civilization. Certainly this is a noble endeavor, whether executed by spider or bee. But as we have discussed, the aim of the Christian is not to contort the kingdom of man such that it can better approximate the kingdom of God (or the utopias of our imagination). No, the Christian is to learn to see herself gathered by Christ to be as his body, gathered together to be storied by the pronouncement of judgment and the heralding of grace—to be a human being with and for others.

But what is a human being? This is the question assumed by the inauguration to this chapter.

It is the question that must position the marks of Christian action (the art of living) *for* our technological age.

Preeminently, Christian *paideia* is a training in the art of living as Christ, whose labors are *for* this world—labors that pronounce *no* such that one might hear afresh the *yes* of God's being-in-act. Rather, in pronouncing *no*, God rejects such sin that promotes alienation from him. Such judgment,

43. Vallor, *Technology and the Virtues*, 76.

however, is not directed at us—instead, Jesus takes the rejection and the *no* of God on himself fully as the vicarious human for all humanity. But the *no* is necessary so that we can hear God's *yes*: Jesus Christ does not encounter the world, and therefore each of us, as "an accuser, as a prosecutor, as a judge, as an executioner." He is "the herald of this Yes which God has spoken to it [the world]. . . . God has loved it from all eternity, and . . . He has put His love into action in the death of Jesus Christ," as Barth puts it.[44] The resurrection of Jesus Christ accordingly signals God's *yes* to Jesus Christ, and therefore to us. In and through Jesus Christ, the *yes* of God is freely given to all human beings—and all human beings are given freedom to return to God as they learn to live in *this* world.

What does this mean for our technological society?

It means that the event of Christ's being has opened a space for persons to become human beings. The divine intention has been to liberate a space where each one, together, might exercise her vocation as a real human being. Thus, the pronouncement of judgment and the heralding of grace is a saying, a summons, that shapes us into the community of the church, conformed toward human being, enabled to see the world *realistically.* This means that we are able to see the world christologically. We are enabled to see the world as a place where suffering, frailty, and limitedness in every noble and ignoble part of being are acknowl-

44. Karl Barth, *Church Dogmatics IV.1*, trans. Gregory W. Bromiley and Thomas F. Torrance (Edinburgh: T&T Clark, 1984), 347.

SAYING, SEEING, BECOMING HUMAN

edged and honored.[45] We are *also* enabled to see the world as
a place where the will to live that promotes the practices to
"improve, raise, and, perhaps, radically transform the general living conditions of all men," perhaps expecting "a new
and quite different order of society, guaranteeing better living conditions for all," is respected.[46] Such a world refuses
isolation (the solitary will) for fellowship (mutual dependence).

This realism, however, must learn to take seriously the
history of the fall of the world and the freedom we have
been given to live in this world. This means that one is to be
trained to see the world as the place where the powers and
principalities too are disunited in their aims, severing meaning and alienating humanity from the earth, their neighbors, and themselves. One must therefore learn to discern
the discontent and to see the essential nature of things,
of technology and of death, for example. Accordingly, one
must learn that a human being is "free to face the world
as it is without flinching, without shock, without fear, with-
out surprise, without embarrassment, without sentimental-
ity, without guile or disguise. [Humanity] is free to live in the
world as it is."[47]

45. Dietrich Bonhoeffer, "Ethics as Formation," in *Ethics*, trans. Reinhard
Krauss, Charles C. West, and Douglas W. Stott, ed. Clifford J. Green,
Dietrich Bonhoeffer Works 6 (Minneapolis: Fortress Press, 2005),
82–100.
46. Karl Barth, *Church Dogmatics*, trans. Geoffrey W. Bromiley and Thomas
F. Torrance (Edinburgh: T&T Clark, 2004), III.4, 363.
47. Stringfellow, *Dissenter in a Great Society*, 161.

To be clear, this "as it is" does not mean that one's creativity ought to be restrained so that the world becomes reified in a particular state, as though the status quo were to be celebrated. No. That too is what we must dissent. Rather, it means that one conformed by Christ is able to live a human life, liberated from the coercive powers that train discontentment and contempt.

The realist therefore is a human being, one who has learned to recognize that the first commands of the decalogue, "You shall have no other gods before me. . . . You shall not make for yourself an idol. . . . You shall not bow down to them or worship them" (Exod 20:3–5 NRSV), are permissions: You *may* not worship other gods. You *may* not fashion idols. You *may* not trust these gods and conform to these idols. "You *may*" means we are liberated from such malforming devotion. The realist accordingly is freed not to be taken captive by chthonic powers, the gods of power and progress, which demean and dehumanize, which alienate and constrain being to its state in our technological age. The human being is liberated to learn about the Christian vocation within this world—to face it as it is rather than to construct an image of an ideal world, an otherworld, a utopia.

This vocation—the freedom to face the world, to gather with both friends and fellows, neighbors both similar and dissimilar, to gather with the earth and its inhabitants—is not to be governed by an ethics that is itself as a technique. Rather, the vocation is a summons to become human beings, to become creative and to seek after wisdom—navigating life without the fear of punishment or the tyranny of purity (both birthed of control over the inner life), learning to play in the world and to delight in others as a disciple of Wisdom (Prov 8:1–31).

It may be, however, that such playfulness and delight will be *inconsistent*. Such inconsistency is an expression of human freedom, which is not bounded by norms, ideals, principles, or preconceived answers.[48] Christian ethics, therefore, as the participation of liberated human beings in this world, is not "settled and stereotyped, uniform and preclusive, neat and predictable."[49] Such ethics are indicative of modern ethical systems and moral techniques, such as those that justify the advancement of novel technologies and instrumental programs by measure of utility. Rather, "The Christian acts in this world and in particular circumstances in a society . . . as an expression of [her] freedom from just such idols."[50]

Freed from such idols, one might be able to learn to see the world as it is. One might be able to see both friends and fellows in their state, beleaguered by war and forced migration, by ecological corruption and species collapse, by profound racism and penal retribution, by unrelenting financial pressures, corporate greed, and unemployment, and by ever-evolving technological development that promises everything and delivers discontent. One might be able to see such fellows in their state, but such vision "does not yield 'right' or 'good' or 'true' or 'ultimate' answers,"[51] as though such problems were objective, able to be mastered,

---

48. Bonhoeffer, "Ethics as Formation," 83.
49. William Stringfellow, *Conscience and Obedience* (Waco, TX: Word Books, 1977), 27.
50. Stringfellow, *Dissenter in a Great Society*, 162.
51. Stringfellow, *Ethic for Christians*, 54.

and were mere analogues of machine parts. Yet, performing solidarity, one might learn to be concerned *for* her neighbor, for all persons, and the diversity of problems, pains, issues, and aches confronted in the fallen world.[52] That is to say, the human vocation, the vocation that pursues freedom, is also *intercessory*. One might be free to learn to "deal with human decision and action in relation to the other creatures, notably the principalities and powers in the very midst of the conflict, distortion, alienation, disorientation, chaos, decadence of the Fall."[53]

Intercession is a reminder of what a human being might be. The witness of intercession demands that we attend to others, both victims and victimizers of poisonous venom, in haste and determination, "to expose the reign of death in Babylon while affirming the aspiration for new life intuitive in all human beings and inherent in all principalities." This too is a humanizing witness: as Stringfellow says, there is "no way to act humanly in isolation from the whole of humanity, no possibility for a person to act humanly without becoming implicated with all other human beings."[54] Such solidarity might resource the strength to endure calamity and crisis. It is a fidelity to wade through despair toward human flourishing. Such intercession might afford the opportunity to stumble into Jerusalem, discovering new possibilities that promote human flourishing.

By such intercession one might relearn the skill to be

---

52. Stringfellow, *Dissenter in a Great Society*, 163.
53. Stringfellow, *Ethic for Christians*, 55.
54. Stringfellow, *Ethic for Christians*, 63, 56.

"technological" *for* the well-being of all things. This, presumably, is eschatologically essential to any sense of the art of living. Such skill, relearned, might be able to abide Adorno's definition of progress freed from profane doctrine: "to think of progress in the crudest, most basic terms: that no one should go hungry anymore, that there should be no more torture, no more Auschwitz. Only then will the idea of progress be free from lies."[55] Such skill might thus reflect the technique of Christ, whose faithfulness trains us toward an active faith reflecting the Matthean pericope (Matt 25:31–46), faith that clothes the naked, feeds the hungry, comforts the distressed, shelters the destitute, cares for the infirmed and imprisoned, and so on.

Our attention, therefore, must be on other human persons and lived needs, rather than the artifacts of technology and their commodities in the first instance. It must be on the state of being that nullifies hope—on the imposition to human flourishing and to essential relationships through the coercive pull of idolatry and the degradation that persists, which generates despair. It must become a humanizing attention. If our attention to artifacts is also required, it must be interrogatory, "admonishing the principalities about their vocation as *creatures* called to serve the social needs of human beings"[56] and not as gods determined to dominate by vainglory.

Thus, we must learn to give our due attention to persons,

55. Theodor Adorno, cited in Detlev Claussen, *Theodor W. Adorno: One Last Genius* (Cambridge, MA: Harvard University Press, 2008), 338.
56. Stringfellow, *Ethic for Christians*, 57 (emphasis added).

those caught up by the allure of technique, but especially those degraded by it. We must learn to deal with human decision and action in relation to these persons, both coerced and degraded by techno-ontology, yet persons possessing creativity, curiosity, and impulsive demands that must be disciplined.

By such performance, we all might be humanized.

When I say "give due attention" and "must deal with," I mean that we *must act* such that we might learn to be(come) human and learn to accept the responsibility to humanize others. Realism, dissent, inconsistency, and intercession are all performative.[57] They are *paideutic* in that way, training us as we participate in them. To live humanly in this fallen world requires that we act in this fallen world, imitating Christ. Such actions do not fall impotent, leaving the world unchanged. Rather, they change everything.

The Christian, therefore, as the one learning to be human, is being conformed to see what she has been gathered into, the body of Christ, the church, which does not labor to bring a kingdom of man, nor does it seek to coerce the world to be(come) the church, but will "continually seek to make the Kingdom of God more concrete and visible in the common life of human beings"[58]—to make it more visible *for* our technological age.

---

57. These marks of Christian involvement come from Stringfellow's essay "The Orthodoxy of Radical Involvement," in *Dissenter in a Great Society*, 161–64. There he presents realism, inconsistency, radicalism, dissent, and intercession as characteristics of the Christian life, therefore human life, in the world.
58. Williams, *Being Disciples*, 73.

Conclusion

As I conclude, let me emphasize this: my aim has not been to issue a generic and totalizing critique of all technological artifacts and advances. Technological progress can in fact be a good thing. The spark of creativity experienced by the progenitors of novel devices and artifacts is indeed a very human and good reality. Moreover, as Marcel reminds his reader, the commodities of technology can open up new possibilities for human flourishing. However, technology as an ontology, as a fallen power, can coerce a misguided gaze and habits of discontent that disconnect us from others and from the self. Technology as an ontology, as I have shown, disturbs our attention to that which has been given. It can resource a sort of anguish that learns to regard the world as that which ought not to be. Confronted by such frustration and despair, confronted by disaffection from others, as from the self, technology as an ontology reveals itself as inadequate to deal with the complexities and totalities of human persons—and not only inadequate but also caustic. Thus, the conditions created by the ontology of technology can become detrimental to and degrade human being. They can work against the formation of the person, of a society of persons, obstructing its fulfillment.

Although much of this volume has labored to critically question the essential nature of technology, to probe an understanding of the ontology of technology, you will not find in these final statements a moralist plea. I will not suggest the answer to the crisis of technology is to be found in the closing of factories or in the dismantling of research-and-development endeavors. It is not to be found in the obstruction of projects and the skills requisite to managing technological artifacts and inventing new ones. The answer is not to be found in the crippling of economic ties to novel artifacts of technology, including those associated with war and violence, which I do abhor. The answer is not to be found in a return to small-scale sustainable farming practices or a renewing of pagan affection for the powers and pixies, spirits and sprites, found in nature. It is not to be found by naive notions of embodiment that reject virtual technologies out of hand and demand forms of engagement that are rudimentary and contrived. Indeed, my argument is not that we should deprive ourselves of the benefits of technology, necessarily. We should not accept these benefits outright, either. None of the characteristics of Christian witness, or the practices of *paideia*, as introduced above, would conclude as such.

Rather, as Donald MacKinnon commends:

It is the duty of the Church to strive, in its members, to bring all things into the captivity of Christ partly because *in themselves* all things demand that subjection if their true nature is to be revealed and expressed.

If this is true of the sphere of the Church it follows equally that any man, whoever he may be, whose concern with his world expresses that crucial quality which will enable him to rest in none of the easy solutions which conveniently ignore some of its profoundest problems, must enter that dimension of existence in which we see the significance of the Empty Tomb. . . .

He is man; "God of the substance of his Father, begotten before all ages; man of the substance of his mother, born into the world." There is no point at which the problem of human living receives so unequivocal a definition as in Jesus, and that because in him is contained the solution. The true nature of the paradoxical situation in which we live as men stands revealed in the light of this representative life and death and in the mighty act of divine power and majesty which is its consummation and the earnest of the consummation of all things.[59]

Captivity to Christ means that we must learn to stay with him. By staying with him, by the habitual repetition of his symbols and signs, we might learn to live humanly. By taking up the way of Christ, we might learn to live in freedom during the fall and to bear witness to human being (becoming) *for* a technological age.

---

59. MacKinnon, "Tomb Was Empty," 259.

Afterword by Brent P. Waters

There are at least two good reasons to read this book. Or more accurately, since this is an afterword, two good reasons for the reader to have spent the time to come this far. *Content* is the first reason. Ashley John Moyse has done a masterful job of describing our contemporary circumstances. The origins and consequences of these circumstances are largely driven by a technological mindset, of which the proliferation of devices and gadgets cluttering our lives discloses a prior—and far more expansive and potentially menacing—commitment to mastering nature and human nature.

Moyse crafts his description in a terse, at times stark, manner, often including understated yet incisive criticism. The net effect is a guide through the thickets of our technological era or emerging technoculture, one suitable for both expert and novice alike. Prominent authors, such as Heidegger, Ellul, Grant, and a host of others, as well as the most pressing moral, social, political, and economic issues, are laced throughout. Yet the names and topics are not addressed in a lockstep fashion that numbs rather than excites the imagination. Rather, the book is a provocative narration that gently forces the reader to engage the dilemma of late modernity as an unavoidable and necessary reality of the human condition. Technology is now such a ubiquitous presence in our daily lives that it cannot be removed without inflicting severe damage, yet we do not know whether the fate of this presence will prove enlivening or deadly. To invoke biblical imagery, there is no going back to Eden, but whether our cherished technology is divine or demonic is unknown. In short, the simple quandary we face as late moderns is that we can't live without technology, but can we live with it?

Unlike many critical accounts of technology, however, *The Art of Living* does not counsel despair. This leads to the second good reason to read this book: its *interrogative tone.* Moyse offers no sweeping denunciation (or endorsement) of technology—as it should be if our present circumstances are to be genuinely engaged. As the dilemma mentioned above suggests, our technological era enframes a deep ambivalence, a simultaneous attraction and revulsion, shaping a culture in which our technical prowess and ingenuity breed both optimism and pessimism about the future. The dilemma, however, cannot be resolved by appealing uncritically to either a bright or dark fate. Rather, posing exacting questions to the sources of both our optimism and pessimism offers the most promising way to negotiate a late-modern cultural landscape—negotiated in a manner that assists the art of living. In this interrogative tone there is a muted hope. To borrow from Hannah Arendt, we must stop and think, and good thinking always begins with good questions.

The book, however, is not a haphazard collection of partially or unanswered questions. There is a thread, sometimes readily apparent and at other times hidden, that holds the book together: anthropology. The question of human flourishing specifically is posed, sometimes overtly and other times covertly, time and again, but with varying emphases—as it should be in any inquiry into artful living. The questions are not developed, much less answered, in a comprehensive way. That is a great value of the book, for Moyse's interrogation invites others to join the inquiry. There is particularly an invitation to develop an anthropology that enables human flourishing in light of our present circumstances. But what is needed is not a generic or bland anthropology, for that would merely reinforce the intellectual laziness often accompanying and shaping the emerging technoculture. No, what is required is a religious anthropology, indeed, an overtly Christian anthropology (if the intellectual taking up the task is Christian) to counter the religious conviction of mastering nature and human nature that underlies the purposes and structures of the present age.

I assume this invitation could be accepted by Christian philosophers who would use core convictions and beliefs in developing systematic and normative accounts of human ontology and the requisite morality derived from being human. More specifically, the question of human flourishing could (and should) be addressed: What must a person be and do to flourish? The same question could (and should) also be asked of social and political forms of human association. Moreover, addressing these and similar questions must take into account our present circumstances of the emerging technoculture. To what extent, for instance, does the attempt to master nature and human nature help or hinder humans from realizing their true being, and subsequently, does such mastery assist or deter human flourishing? In developing such an anthropology, the Christian philosopher would presumably, in part, draw on the doctrines of creation and eschatology to simultaneously ground humans in a divinely created and ordered creation heading, over time, toward its divinely appointed destiny.

Admittedly, such a simple scheme does not eliminate a host of issues preventing human flourishing, such as failing to align oneself, or one's social and political associations, with this trajectory. To invoke an old and unpopular word, the problem of sin must be included in any anthropology, especially one purporting to be Christian. Accepting this invitation may appear daunting, perhaps too daunting given the ascendant secularizing and anti-Christian forces dominating late modernity. This is understandable given the close alliance between these forces and proponents of extensive technological development. For any normative anthropology can only serve to limit the mastery of nature and human nature.

Nonetheless, the invitation must be accepted by philosophers qualified to undertake this daunting task, if for no other reason than to dispel the dangerous fiction of "technological neutrality." Since the appetite for mastery is effectively insatiable, harm is the only criterion that may block the development and use of a technology. If it can be demonstrated that users or bystanders, and increasingly the environment, are already or will likely be harmed by a technology, then its unwarranted use can be restricted or prohibited. But there are two caveats. First, many, if not most, technologies have inherent risks but are judged to be acceptable. Automobiles and commercial airplanes are two such examples. Second, some technologies are lethal but regarded as necessary to protect and preserve order when used by the right people for the right reasons. For instance, weapons may be used to deter, disable, or kill criminals. Yet if there is no normative standard of what humans should be and do, then harm (and flourishing) in most instances is reduced to a subjective determination. Ten hours a day using social media does not harm me or anyone else. Really? Or worse, those in a position of power to do so determine what constitutes harm or acceptable risk and impose this determination on the weak. Young people should not be allowed to smoke, but they may drive cars or serve as military combatants.

Yet, in both instances avoiding harm does not necessarily promote flourishing. Consequently, many technologies are devices or methods that serve as distractions enabling the passing of time. As distractions, technologies are hardly neutral, since users and bystanders must alter who they are and what they must do in order to avail themselves of the proffered benefits. Such required alterations in being and doing is a strange understanding of neutrality. As George Grant recognizes, the comforting adage of a computer scientist that the computer does not impose the ways it should be used is nonsense. Of course it imposes; otherwise it could not be a computer. In the absence of a normative anthropology that serves as a measuring standard, flourishing and harm are in large part rendered vacuous.

I also assume this invitation could be accepted by Christian theologians. The task undertaken by the theologian would include many, if not all, the elements of a normative anthropology as noted in the preceding paragraphs. The theologian, like the philosopher, must ascribe what humans should be and do as commanded or ordained by their creator. The chief difference between the theologian and philosopher is one of emphasis. Whereas the philosopher is primarily concerned with developing a systematic anthropology as informed by core convictions, the attention of the theologian is principally focused on the doctrinal or dogmatic veracity of the core convictions in play. In constructing or clarifying relevant doctrinal or dogmatic teaching, the theologian has a wide range of hermeneutical and expository tools at her disposal, such as Scripture, tradition, reason, and experience.

Consequently, a pressing issue for the theologian is where to begin; which doctrine or dogma best lends itself to developing a theological and normative anthropology that could promote the art of living within the emerging technoculture? The answer is not as evident as might be assumed. The doctrine of creation in general, and the creation of human beings in particular, seems to be the obvious place to start. There many theologians ground their respective anthropologies. The result, however, is not always entirely satisfying. For instance, much could be written about what it means to be human and what is thereby required of humans to do in the context of our present circumstances. Such theological narratives may prove insightful or edifying, but not necessarily distinctively Christian. The resulting anthropology may include a veneer of Christian rhetoric, but the façade is often thin, barely disguising a core of generic religious claims. The resulting critique of the attempt at mastering nature and human nature, then, is little more than an expression of the theologian's ideological platitudes masquerading as doctrinal or dogmatic teaching. Or worse, creation is used as a starting point but is collapsed into an odd synonym for a pristine but unrecognizable nature. The resulting environmental or green theology is then dedicated to either recovering Eden or enabling so-called cocreators to work with God in somehow directing nature toward a favorable end that cannot be known in advance by either God or his cadre of cocreators in an indeterminant creation. In such a scheme, the mastery of nature and human nature is effectively preserved, albeit in a kinder, gentler, and environmentally friendly way, and Christian teaching may or may not serve as a rhetorical device depending on the immediate audience.

What would be a better doctrinal or dogmatic place to begin for a normative anthropology that is inimitably Christian? Perhaps Christology, the incarnation in particular. To the best of my knowledge, no other religion asserts as an indispensable article of faith that the word of God became flesh, became a human creature. Other religions and mythologies have their divine-human hybrids, but none are identified simultaneously as the origin, savior, and end of creation. Yet this is precisely what the incarnation teaches. The incarnate word is the one word, the three-in-one God, that creates, redeems, and fulfills all that is material, temporal, and finite. It is a core conviction that is uniquely Christian.

But what difference might an incarnational anthropology make in assessing and perhaps challenging prevalent attempts at mastering nature and human nature? One possibility suggests itself, namely, that the incarnation affirms and serves as a reminder that humans are finite, mortal, and thereby limited creatures. Mastery plays no role in asserting their divinely appointed role of dominion and stewardship. This does not imply that nothing needs to be done to make creation a habitat suitable for promoting human flourishing. Eden, after all, is not a wilderness but a garden requiring tending. In this respect the sins inhibiting human flourishing are those of both commission and omission. On the one hand, humans may attempt to transform creation into an artifact of their own ingenuity, using technology to commit the sin of pride. On the other hand, humans may fail to take protective or precautionary measures against harmful natural vagaries, idolizing nature in committing the sin of sloth.

The constraints of this afterword do not allow even a brief foray into how an incarnational anthropology might shape a Christian engagement with the predominant technoculture. But again, one possible avenue of inquiry suggests itself. Rejecting the mastery of nature and human nature does not sanction any wholesale rejection of technology. The incarnation affirms the physical and embodied nature of human creatures. Consequently, technologies can and should be deployed that enhance the physical and material well-being of people. But humans are also social creatures. As the Bible attests, it is not good for people to be alone. Technologies can and should be resisted when they serve to isolate and alienate us from each other. FaceTime I suppose, has its value, but it is no substitute for face-to-face conversation.

The most pressing challenge of our contemporary circumstances is, I believe, to find that balance between addressing the needs of finite, mortal, and therefore embodied beings in efficacious ways, but also in ways that do not wither the already fragile social bonds of creaturely imperfection that bind humans together. A fitting Christian anthropology has potentially much to offer in finding this balance. Ashley Moyse has taken some initial and highly promising steps in crafting such an anthology, and he has invited others to join him in this work. I hope his invitation is accepted.

Brent P. Waters
Jerre and Mary Joy Stead Professor of Christian Social Ethics
Garrett-Evangelical Theological Seminary

Select Bibliography

Berdyaev, Nicholas. *The Fate of Man in the Modern World*. Translated by Donald Lowrie. San Rafael, CA: Semantron, 2009.

Brague, Rémi. *Curing Mad Truths: Medieval Wisdom for the Modern Age*. Notre Dame: University of Notre Dame Press, 2019.

———. *The Kingdom of Man: Genesis and Failure of the Modern Project*. Translated by Paul Seaton. Notre Dame: University of Notre Dame Press, 2018 [*Le Régne de l'Homme: Genése et échec du projet moderne*. Paris: Gallimard, 2015].

Burdett, Michael S. *Eschatology and the Technological Future*. New York: Routledge, 2014.

Casserley, J. V. Langmead. *The Fate of Modern Culture*. Signposts 1. Westminster, UK: Dacre, 1940.

Ellul, Jacques. *Perspectives on Our Age*. Translated by Joachim Neugroschel. Edited by William H. Vanderburg. New York: Seabury, 1981.

———. *Propaganda: The Formation of Men's Attitudes*. Translated by Konrad Kellen and Jean Lerner. New York: Vintage Books, 1973.

———. *The Technological Society*. Translated by John Wilkinson. New York: Vintage Books, 1964.

Franklin, Ursula. *The Real World of Technology*. CBC Massey Lectures. Montreal: CBC Enterprise, 1990. Rev. ed., Toronto: House of Anansi, 1999.

Frye, Northrop. *The Educated Imagination*. CBC Massey Lectures. Toronto: House of Anansi, 2002.

Grant, George. *Technology and Empire*. Pages 479–594 in *Collected Works of George Grant*. Vol. 3, *(1960-1969)*. Edited by Arthur Davis and Henry Roper. Toronto: Toronto University Press, 2005.

———. *Technology and Justice*. Pages 588–701 in *Collected Works of George Grant*. Vol. 4, *(1970-1988)*. Edited by Arthur Davis and Henry Roper. Toronto: Toronto University Press, 2009.

Guardini, Romano. *The End of the Modern World*. Wilmington, DE: ISI Books, 2013.

Hauerwas, Stanley. *Working with Words: On Learning to Speak Christian*. Eugene, OR: Cascade Books, 2011.

Heidegger, Martin. *The Question Concerning Technology and Other Essays*. Translated by William Lovitt. New York: Harper & Row, 1977.

Horkheimer, Max, and Theodor W. Adorno. *The Dialectic of Enlightenment*. Translated by John Cumming. New York: Continuum, 1996.

Jaeger, Werner. *Early Christianity and Greek Paideia*. Cambridge, MA: Belknap, 1961.

Jonas, Hans. "Towards a Philosophy of Technology." *Hastings Center Report* (February 1979): 34–43.

Marcel, Gabriel. *Man against Mass Society*. Translated by G. S. Fraser. South Bend, IN: St. Augustine's, 2008.

Marcuse, Herbert. *One Dimensional Man*. London: Routledge, 2007.

McKenny, Gerald. *To Relieve the Human Condition: Bioethics, Technology, and the Body*. Albany: State University of New York Press, 1997.

Mesthene, Emmanuel G. *Technological Change: Its Impact on Man and Society*. New York: New American Library, 1970.

Mumford, Lewis. *The Myth of the Machine: The Pentagon of Power*. New York: Harcourt Brace Jovanovich, 1964.

———. *Technics and Civilization*. London: Routledge & Sons, 1934.

Ott, Kate. *Christian Ethics for a Digital Society*. London: Rowman & Littlefield, 2018.

Stringfellow, William. *Dissenter in a Great Society*. Eugene, OR: Wipf & Stock, 2005.

———. *An Ethic for Christians and Other Aliens in a Strange Land*. Eugene, OR: Wipf & Stock, 2004.

Szerszinski, Bronislaw. *Nature, Technology, and the Sacred*. Malden, MA: Blackwell, 2005.

Vallor, Shannon. *Technology and the Virtues: A Philosophical Guide to a Future Worth Wanting*. Oxford: Oxford University Press, 2016.

Williams, Rowan. *Being Disciples: Essentials of the Christian Life*. London: SPCK, 2016.

———. *Being Human: Bodies, Minds, Persons*. London: SPCK, 2018.

Zimmermann, Jens, ed. *Re-envisioning Christian Humanism: Education and the Restoration of Humanity*. Oxford: Oxford University Press, 2016.

Select Index